MICHAEL J H TAYLOR
& JOHN W R TAYLOR

Helicopters of the World

D1271660

Charles Scribner's Sons
NEW YORK

Foreword

According to many aircraft engineers, the helicopter is a misbegotten device that offends against all the finer laws of aerodynamics and structures. Such feelings have been expressed for at least seventy years; and even the Wright brothers, who were first to fly a powered aeroplane, had no love for wings that rotated. In a letter to a friend, in January 1906, Wilbur Wright commented: 'Like all novices we began with the helicopter (in childhood), but soon saw that it had no future and dropped it. The helicopter does with great labour only what the balloon does without labour, and is no more fitted than the balloon for rapid horizontal flight. If its engine stops it must fall with deathly violence, for it can neither float like the balloon nor glide like the aeroplane. The helicopter is much easier to design than the aeroplane but it is worthless when done.'

One of America's greatest inventors of that period took a diametrically opposite view. After a few disparaging glances at the Wright biplane and its stick-and-string contemporaries, Thomas Alva Edison proclaimed: 'The aeroplane won't amount to a damn until they get a machine that will act like a humming bird — go straight up, go forward, go backward, come straight down and alight like a humming bird.'

The gentle genius who proved both men wrong was Igor Sikorsky. By designing, building and flying the first four-engined aeroplane in 1913, and going on to produce the amphibians and flying-boats with which the young Pan American Airways extended its wings over the Pacific and Atlantic Oceans in the 1920s and 30s, he helped to demonstrate the commercial potential of fixed-wing aeroplanes. Then, by perfecting the now-conventional 'single-rotor' helicopter in 1939-40, he gave substance to Edison's concept of a machine that would take off and land vertically, and hover.

Sikorsky believed that helicopters would be used as vehicles to save and to enrich life. In the years that followed World War 2, the industry he founded began supplying small helicopters for experimental passenger and mail services, for ambulance duty, and for spraying chemicals over crops to destroy insect pests and to control plant diseases. The cost was high in monetary terms, but often the human lives and the crops could have been saved in no other way. Then came another war, in Korea. Front-line areas were frequently inaccessible to anything but helicopters. By evacuating wounded men from such places, helicopters reduced to the lowest percentage in military history the number of injured who died. On the outward journeys they carried supplies and ammunition.

The war in Korea established the helicopter as a front-line military type. Its nickname of 'chopper' still reflected the noisy beat of its rotor rather than anything more sinister; but the next American war, in Vietnam, changed this. The Vietcong became so adept at shooting down troop-carrying helicopters that UH-1 Iroquois of the US Army were fitted with guns and rockets to 'keep down the heads' of any Vietcong waiting in the drop zone. It was but a short step to the specialised HueyCobra gunship and, meanwhile, helicopters were fast superseding fixed-wing types as ship-based anti-submarine hunter-killers.

A glance through this book will show how far the 'chopper' has advanced towards and beyond Igor Sikorsky's dream of a life-saving and life-enriching aircraft. Mixed in with the attack helicopters are ambulances, agricultural sprayer-dusters, survey aircraft, flying cranes and a host of other designs that would have earned his full approval. Economics still rule out commercial helicopters in most places where aeroplanes can take off and land; but only 'choppers' can operate to small platforms on offshore oil rigs and to city-centre rooftops; and only 'choppers' can haul frightened people to safety from those same rooftops when buildings catch fire, or from mountain ledges or sinking ships.

No other category of aircraft offers greater variety of shape and size. At one extreme is the huge twin-rotor Soviet V-12, which has lifted a 40-ton load in record attempts. Very different is the tiny RotorWay Scorpion, which anyone can build and fly at home. Nor should modern autogyros be overlooked. They lack the helicopter's complete ability to take off vertically and hover, but bring down costs even further. For that reason they are included in this book, which describes and illustrates all significant helicopters and rotorcraft under development, in production and in service throughout the world. No other book, at any price, offers such complete coverage.

MJHT
JWRT

Aérospatiale SA 316B Alouette III and SA 319B Alouette III Astazou

France

General-purpose, armed reconnaissance, anti-tank and anti-submarine helicopter, in production and service.

Data: SA 319B Alouette III Astazou
Powered by: One 870 shp Turboméca Astazou XIV turboshaft (derated to 600 shp)
Rotor diameter: 36 ft 1 ¾ in (11.02 m)
Length: 32 ft 10 ¾ in (10.03 m)
Empty weight: 2,442 lb (1,108 kg)
Gross weight: 4,960 lb (2,250 kg)
Max speed: 136 mph (220 km/h)
Range: 375 miles (605 km) with six passengers
Accommodation: Pilot and six passengers, two stretchers and two attendants, freight or armament, as described below
Armament: Provision for a 7.62 mm machine-gun, 20 mm gun, four AS.11 or two AS.12 air-to-surface missiles, rocket pods, two Mk 44 homing torpedoes or Hot anti-tank missiles

Photograph: (above) Alouette III of the French Army, carrying four AS 11 missiles
Photograph: (right) SA 316B

The Alouette III was evolved as a larger and more powerful partner for the earlier Alouette II. It can be used for a wide variety of civil and military duties, the former including passenger transport, flight training, ambulance work, and internal and external freight carrying (up to 1,650 lb; 750 kg on external sling on the SA 316B). Military versions can be used for assault, troop transport, reconnaissance, anti-submarine, anti-tank, rescue and other duties. The prototype, designated SA 3160, flew for the first time on February 28, 1959, and this version

remained in production until 1969. It was followed from 1970 by the SA 316B, with the same Turboméca Artouste IIIB turboshaft, derated to 570 shp, but with a strengthened transmission and increased weights. A variant is the SA 319B (described above), with an Astazou XIV engine which gives better all-round performance and reduces fuel consumption by about 25 per cent. Production of the SA 316B and SA 319B continues in France, and the Alouette III is manufactured under licence in India, Pakistan, Romania and Switzerland. Deliveries totalled 1,356, for operation in 69 countries, by the spring of 1976. They include an anti-submarine version known as the Alouette III/ASM, which was adopted by the French Aéronavale in 1974 and serves with Flottille 34F, formed at BAN de Lanvéoc-Poulmic to provide detached flights for service on board anti-submarine corvettes and frigates of the French Navy.

Aérospatiale SA 318C Alouette II Astazou and SA 315B Lama/Cheetah

France

General-purpose helicopters, Alouette II Astazou in service and Lama in production and service.

Data: SA 318C Alouette II Astazou
Powered by: One 530 shp Turboméca Astazou IIA turboshaft (derated to 360 shp)
Rotor diameter: 33 ft 5 ½ in (10.20 m)
Fuselage length: 31 ft 11¾ in (9.75 m) with tail-rotor turning
Empty weight: 1,961 lb (890 kg)
Gross weight: 3,630 lb (1,650 kg)
Max speed: 127 mph (205 km/h)
Range: 447 miles (720 km) with max fuel at S/L
Accommodation: Pilot and four passengers, or two stretchers and medical attendant, or equipment for photographic, observation, agricultural, rescue, flying crane (600 kg payload) and other roles

Photograph: (above) SA 318C Alouette II fitted with pontoons
Photograph: (right) SA 315B Lama

First flown on January 31, 1961, the SA 318C Alouette II Astazou was evolved from the earlier SE 313B Alouette II. Production was completed in 1975, after more than 350 SA 318Cs had been delivered for civil operation in many countries and for service with the French Army. They can be flown with the standard skid, high skid or pneumatic float landing gear.

The Lama is basically an Alouette II fitted with a Turboméca Artouste IIIB turboshaft engine, derated to 570 shp, and the rotor system of the SA 316B Alouette III. The normal maximum take-off weight is raised to 4,300 lb (1,950 kg) and it can perform all the varied duties of the Alouette II, although the payload that can be carried in a flying crane configuration is much greater at 2,200 lb (1,000 kg). Evolved originally as a general-purpose helicopter for the Indian services, the Lama made its maiden flight on March 17, 1969, receiving its French airworthiness certificate some eighteen months later. A Lama established a height record for helicopters on June 21, 1972, by attaining an altitude of 40,820 ft (12,440 m). By early 1976, orders for 184 Lamas had been received from 22 countries; the type is also built as the Cheetah by Hindustan Aeronautics Ltd at the company's Bangalore Complex Helicopter Division. Initial production in India utilised French-built components, and the first Cheetah flew on October 6, 1972. About 20 had been delivered by 1975, and examples built entirely from local materials are due for completion in the latter part of 1976.

Photograph: SA 321L of the South African Air
Force

Aérospatiale SA 321 Super Frelon

France

Commercial and military transport, heavy assault and anti-submarine helicopter, in production and service.

Powered by: Three 1,550 shp Turboméca Turmo IIIC6 turboshafts (Turmo IIIE6 in SA 321H version)
Rotor diameter: 62 ft 0 in (18.90 m)
Fuselage length: 63 ft 7 ¾ in (19.40 m)
Empty weight (SA 321 Ja): 15,141 lb (6,868 kg)
Gross weight: 28,660 lb (13,000 kg)
Cruising speed: 155 mph (249 km/h)
Range: 509 miles (820 km)
Accommodation: Crew of two plus up to 37 passengers (SA 321F); or 27 passengers, or 8,818 lb (4,000 kg) of internal or 11,023 lb (5,000 kg) of externally-slung freight (SA 321Ja); or 30 troops or 15 stretchers and two attendants or freight (SA 321H); or anti-submarine equipment (SA 321G; see below)
Armament (SA 321G): Anti-submarine attack weapons, including four homing torpedoes in pairs on each side of the cabin

Photograph: SA 321G of Flottille 32F, Aéronavale

The Super Frelon is produced for both civil and military applications and is the largest helicopter yet built in France. It was developed from the smaller Frelon, of which two prototypes were built. Sikorsky of America helped with its design through a technical collaboration contract, including the design and testing of the rotor systems, and this led to the Sikorsky-type amphibious hull and stabilising floats (on appropriate versions). The first prototype to fly was a troop transport, which made its maiden flight on December 7, 1962, powered by 1,320 shp Turmo IIIC2 engines. This subsequently set up a helicopter speed record of 217.77 mph (350.47 km/h) over a 15/25 km course, which was not

beaten until 1970, by the Sikorsky Blackhawk. The second prototype, which flew on May 28, 1963, was a naval version. A total of 91 aircraft had been sold by the beginning of 1976, for operation in France and eight other countries, including service with the armed forces of the Chinese People's Republic (SA 321J), Israel (SA 321K transports), Libya (transports) and South Africa (SA 321L transports). Current versions are the SA 321F commercial helicopter, which accommodates 34 to 37 passengers; the SA 321G anti-submarine version, which was the initial production type, first delivered in 1966 to provide support for the French *Redoutable* class submarines while at their home base; the SA 321H military transport, without stabilising floats or external fairings on the lower fuselage; and the SA 321Ja utility transport helicopter, of which the prototype first flew on July 6, 1967.

On anti-submarine missions with the French Navy, Super Frelons operate normally in tactical formations of three or four aircraft, each carrying a full complement of detection, tracking and attack equipment.

Aérospatiale SA 360 Dauphin

France

General-purpose helicopter, in production and service.

Powered by: One 1,050 shp Turboméca Astazou XVIIIA turboshaft
Rotor diameter: 37 ft 8 ¾ in (11.50 m)
Fuselage length: 36 ft 4 in (11.07 m)
Empty weight: 3,428 lb (1,555 kg)
Gross weight: 6,173 lb (2,800 kg)
Max speed: 196 mph (315 km/h)
Range: 405 miles (650 km)
Accommodation: Crew of one or two plus up to 11 passengers, four stretchers and an attendant, six passengers and freight, internal or external freight (up to 2,500 lb/1,150 kg internally, 3,300 lb/1,500 kg externally), 4/5 passengers in executive configuration, or other equipment including weapons.
Armament: Military version has provision for a Minitat underfuselage gun turret and six or eight Hot air-to-surface anti-tank missiles

Designed to supersede the Alouette III as a commercial and military helicopter, the first SA 360 Dauphin prototype made its maiden flight on June 2, 1972, powered by a 980 shp Turboméca Astazou XVI engine; 180 flights were made in this configuration. The second prototype flew on January 29, 1973, and on May 4 the original prototype resumed flying in a modified form.

The Astazou XVI engine had been replaced by an Astazou XVIIIA; other changes included the fitting of weights to the rotor blades to reduce vibration and eliminate ground resonance. During the next two weeks this prototype set up three speed records in Class E1d, averaging 185.8 mph (299 km/h) over a 100 km closed circuit, 193.9 mph (312 km/h) over 3 km, and 188.3 mph (303 km/h) over 15 km, all with a load equivalent to eight passengers. By 1974, the two prototypes had logged over 400 hours in flight. The first production SA 360 made its first flight in April 1975. Deliveries were scheduled to begin in early 1976, at which time 26 had been ordered.

Aérospatiale SA 365 Dauphin

France

General-purpose helicopter, under development.

Powered by: Two 650 shp Turboméca Arriel free-turbine turboshafts
Rotor diameter: 37 ft 8¾ in (11.50 m)
Fuselage length: 36 ft 4 in (11.07 m)
Gross weight: 7,055 lb (3,200 kg)
Max speed: approximately 196 mph (315 km/h)
Range: 357 miles (575 km)
Accommodation: Crew of one or two and up to 11 passengers, four stretchers and an attendant, six passengers and freight, internal or external freight, 4/5 passengers in executive configuration, or other equipment including weapons (see below)
Armament: Military version may have provision for a Minitat underfuselage gun turret and six or eight Hot air-to-surface anti-tank missiles

First flown on January 24, 1975, the SA 365 Dauphin is a twin-engined version of the Aérospatiale SA 360 Dauphin. It differs from the latter in several other ways. There is no clutch in the output rotor drive from each of the engines into the main gearbox, as the engines are free-turbines; the horizontal stabiliser has inverted-camber aerofoil section; the vertical tail fins are offset; and the upper fuselage has a new fairing which extends from the engines to the tailboom. Gross weight is some 880 lb greater than that of the SA 360, although the maximum speed remains about the same. Production of the SA 365 is due to begin in 1976/77, the first order having been received from International Air Taxi of Anchorage, Alaska. Orders totalled 23 in March 1976.

On January 28, 1975, a variant of this helicopter was flown for the first time, powered by two 590 shp Avco Lycoming LTS 101 turboshafts. It was designated SA 366, but no production of this model will be undertaken.

Aérospatiale SE 313B Alouette II

France

Civil and military general-purpose helicopter, in service.

Powered by: One 530 shp Turboméca Artouste IIC6 turboshaft (derated to 360 shp)
Rotor diameter: 33 ft 6 in (10.20 m)
Length: 31 ft 9 in (9.66 m) overall with blades folded
Empty weight: 1,973 lb (895 kg)
Gross weight: 3,527 lb (1,600 kg)
Max speed: 115 mph (185 km/h)
Range: 62-186 miles (100-300 km)
Accommodation: Pilot and four passengers, two stretchers and an attendant, or freight

The SE 313B was the first production version of the Alouette range of helicopters that were originated by the former Sud-Est company. Two prototype Alouette IIs were built, designated SE 3120s and powered by Salmson 9 piston engines, and these were developed for agricultural spraying. The production version, originally designated SE 3130 and then redesignated SE 313B, was first delivered for military use in 1957, some two years after the prototype Alouette II had flown on March 12, 1955. Production of the SE 313B totalled 923 aircraft; these were operated by a total of 33 countries, of which 22 put the aircraft into military service. Military operators included the French Army, West German armed forces, British Army, and the armed forces of Austria, Belgium, Cambodia, Congo, Dominican Republic, Indonesia, Israel, Ivory Coast, Laos, Lebanon, Mexico, Morocco, Netherlands, Peru, Portugal, South Africa, Sweden, Switzerland and Tunisia. SE 313Bs have been used for a variety of roles, including passenger and freight transport, liaison, close support, observation, rescue, casualty evacuation, photography, flying-crane and agricultural work.

Aérospatiale/Westland SA 330 Puma   France/Great Britain

Assault and civil transport helicopter, in production and service.

Data: SA 330B and E
Powered by: Two 1,320 shp Turboméca Turmo IIIC4 turboshafts
Rotor diameter: 49 ft 2 ½ in (15.00 m)
Fuselage length: 48 ft 1 ½ in (14.06 m)
Empty weight: 7,403 lb (3,358 kg)
Gross weight: 14,110 lb (6,400 kg)
Max speed: 174 mph (281 km/h) at sea level
Max range: 390 miles (620 km) with standard fuel
Accommodation: Crew of 2 and 16-20 troops, six stretchers and four seated patients, or freight

Photograph: SA 330B of EH 1/68 'Pyrénées'

Available in both civil and military versions, the SA 330 was developed by Aérospatiale (then Sud-Aviation) originally to fulfil a requirement of the French Army for a medium-size helicopter that would be able to operate in all weathers and climates in the tactical assault and transport roles. The first of two prototypes and six pre-production aircraft flew on April 15, 1965, followed in September 1968 by the first production helicopter. Meanwhile, in 1967, the RAF had chosen the SA 330 for its Tactical Transport Programme and ordered forty. In the following year, the SA 330 became one of three helicopters included in an Anglo-French production programme; Westland Helicopters became responsible for certain components and for the assembly of the 40 RAF helicopters. The first Westland-produced example, designated SA 330E Puma HC Mk 1, flew on November 25, 1970; the first RAF unit to be formed was No 33 Squadron, in 1971, followed by No 230

Squadron in 1972. The first French Army unit had become operational in June 1970, and orders for this service totalled 130. The French Air Force also ordered nine. The export military versions, designated SA 330C and H, are used in several countries, including Algeria, Chile, Portugal, South Africa, Belgium, Abu Dhabi, Ivory Coast and Zaire. They are powered by two 1,400 shp Turboméca Turmo IVB or two 1,575 shp Turmo IVC turboshafts respectively.

The first example of the SA 330F and G civil versions was flown on September 26, 1969, and initial production aircraft were powered by 1,435 shp Turmo IVA engines. Since 1973, the SA 330G has been fitted with Turmo IVCs. By March 1976, total sales of the SA 330 Puma stood at 453, and production continues at between six and ten helicopters a month.

Note: Further illustration on page 12

Aérospatiale SA 330G (See page 11)

Aérospatiale/Westland SA 341 and SA 342 Gazelle

France/Great Britain

Military and civil utility helicopters, in production and service.

Data: SA 341G
Powered by: One 590 shp Turboméca Astazou IIIA turboshaft
Rotor diameter: 34 ft 5 ½ in (10.50 m)
Fuselage length: 31 ft 3 ¼ in (9.53 m)
Empty weight: 2,022 lb (917 kg)
Gross weight: 3,970 lb (1,800 kg)
Max speed: 192 mph (310 km/h)
Range: 416 miles (670 km)
Accommodation: Crew of one or two and three passengers, two stretchers or freight
Armament: Provision on military versions for a variety of armament, which can include four AS.11, four Hot, two AS.12 or four TOW missiles, two pods for 36 mm rockets, 7.62 mm machine-guns, General Electric Minigun, Emerson Minitat or chin turret

Photograph: (bottom left) SA 341B Gazelle AH Mk 1
Photograph: (below) SA 342, with underfuselage Minitat multi-barrel machine-gun turret extended

The Gazelle is one of three helicopters covered under production agreements between Aérospatiale and Westland, signed in 1967. The first of two prototype SA 340 Gazelles made its maiden flight in France on April 7, 1967. The prototypes were followed by four pre-production aircraft, the third of which was to British Army requirements. The first pre-production aircraft set up three records in Class E1c on May 13/14, 1971, including 193.9 mph (312 km/h) over a 15/25 km straight course. The second pre-production Gazelle was subsequently fitted with a 650 shp Turboméca Arriel engine and was used as a test aircraft. On August 6, 1971, the first production SA 341 Gazelle flew, with an uprated Turboméca Astazou IIIA engine, longer cabin and larger tail unit. British variants of the Gazelle, assembled at Yeovil, are the British Army SA 341B (designated Gazelle AH. Mk 1) with a 600 shp Astazou IIIN engine, of which 138 were ordered for the Army and Marines; the SA 341C (designated HT. Mk 2), 30 ordered for the Royal Navy; and the SA 341D (HT. Mk 3), 13 ordered for the RAF. Other versions include the SA 341F, with the Astazou IIIC engine, of which 166 are to be acquired by the French Army; the SA 341H export version, powered by the Astazou IIIB engine and licence-built in Yugoslavia; and the SA 342 variant for Kuwait with an 870 shp Astazou XIVH engine. The civil variant of the Gazelle is the SA 341G; it was this version that became the first type of helicopter authorised to be flown by a single pilot under IFR Cat 1 conditions, with 1,800 ft forward vision and a ceiling of 200 ft. By the spring of 1976, 718 Gazelles had been sold, to operate in 20 different countries.

Agusta A 109   Italy

General-purpose helicopter, in production and service.

Powered by: Two 420 shp Allison 250-C20B turboshafts
Rotor diameter: 36 ft 1 in (11.00 m)
Fuselage length: 36 ft 0 ¾ in (10.99 m)
Empty weight: 2,998 lb (1,360 kg)
Gross weight: 5,400 lb (2,450 kg)
Max speed: 174 mph (280 km/h)
Range: up to 438 miles (705 km)
Accommodation: Crew of one or two, plus six passengers and baggage, or two stretchers and two medical attendants (with one pilot only) or freight. Can also be equipped for other roles, including rescue and attack
Armament: Attack version can have a 7.62 mm Minitat or twin MG-3 machine-guns. Optional pylons for two rocket pods, each containing seven/eighteen SNIA rockets. Four TOW or AS.11 anti-tank missiles

Designed with a distinct "Bell Helicopters" look about it—perhaps reflecting the fact that Agusta and Bell have had close manufacturing links since 1952—the first of three prototype A 109s flew on August 4, 1971. It had been conceived as a high-performance general-purpose helicopter, and production began with an initial batch of ten aircraft, delivery of which was scheduled to begin in late 1975. In 1976 five A 109s were to begin evaluation trials with the Italian Army, armed with TOW anti-tank missiles. Further development of the design has already been initiated, in the form of a mock-up armed helicopter designated A 129.

The fuselage of the A 109 is built in four sections, comprising the nose, cockpit, main cabin and tailboom. The two engines are mounted above the rear cabin, side-by-side, and drive a four-blade main rotor. Interior layout is flexible, to enable the helicopter to adapt to its many roles. Thus, the forward bulkhead of the cabin is removable to allow the full complement of two stretchers and two attendants to be carried when on ambulance duty. Similarly, for freight carrying, the front three seats in the passenger cabin can be removed. Provision for auxiliary fuel tanks will enable the A 109 to perform long-endurance search and rescue missions.

Agusta-Bell 204 (Bell 204 and Fuji 204B/204B-2)

Italy (and USA, Japan)

Military and commercial utility helicopter and anti-submarine helicopter, in production and service.

Data: Agusta-Bell 204
Powered by: One Rolls-Royce Gnome H.1200 or Lycoming T53 or General Electric T58 turboshaft
Rotor diameter: 48 ft 0 in (14.63 m), or 44 ft 0 in (13.41 m)
Fuselage length: 41 ft 7 in (12.67 m)
Empty weight (military utility version): 6,481 lb (2,940 kg)
Gross weight with armament: 9,500 lb (4,310 kg)
Cruising speed (ASW mission): 104 mph (167 km/h)
Accommodation: Pilot and nine passengers or freight. Can be used for other roles, including air

ambulance and rescue, and can carry armament
Armament: Armament can include two Mk 44 torpedoes, or AS.12 or similar missiles on multi-role version

Photograph: (above) Agusta-Bell AB-204AS of the Italian Navy
Photograph: (below) Fuji-Bell 204B of Tokyo Metropolitan Police

Bell produced the Model 204 in both military and civil variants; the military versions for the US Army appear under the "Bell UH-1 Iroquois" entry. The commercial version produced by Bell was the Model 204B, corresponding to the UH-1B, and was powered by a 1,100 shp Lycoming T5311A engine. The Model 204B was also built by Agusta from 1961, and over 250 had been delivered by the close

of production in 1974. These were supplied to Italy (armed forces and for commercial operation), Austria (military), Ethiopia (military), Kuwait (military), Holland (military), Lebanon (commercial), Saudi Arabia (military), Norway (commercial), Spain (military), Sweden (military and commercial), Switzerland (commercial) and Turkey (military). Agusta also designed and produced an anti-submarine version, designated Agusta-Bell 204AS, powered by a 1,290 shp General Electric T58-GE-3 engine. Delivered to the Italian and Spanish navies, it is an all-weather helicopter, with sonar linked to the automatic stabilisation and automatic approach to hovering equipment, and can be fitted with AN/APN-195 search radar and torpedoes. A version of the 204AS, equipped with

Bendix search radar and air-to-surface missiles, can also be used against surface ships.

Fuji of Japan has manufactured the Model 204 in three main versions—the 204B and 204B-2 commercial helicopters and the UH-1B for the Japanese Army. By 1973, Fuji had delivered 90 UH-1B helicopters to the Army; in the following year six were evaluated in attack configuration, each carrying two pods for 70 mm rockets.

Twenty-three 204B commercial helicopters had been delivered by Fuji to eight operators by early 1975, seven of them for Police use. The first example of the 204B-2 was acquired by the Asahi Helicopter Co in 1974. Powered by a 1,400 shp Kawasaki-built Lycoming T53-K-13B engine, this has a tractor-type tail rotor.

Agusta-Bell 206 JetRanger   Italy

Anti-submarine, attack and general-purpose military helicopter; and light civil helicopter, in production and service.

Data: AB 206B-1
Powered by: One 400 shp Allison 250-C20 turboshaft (derated to 317 shp)
Rotor diameter: 35 ft 4 in (10.77 m)
Fuselage length: 32 ft 4 in (9.85 m)
Empty weight: 1,540 lb (698 kg)
Max gross weight: 3,350 lb (1,519 kg)
Max speed: 138 mph (222 km/h)
Endurance: 3 ½ hours
Accommodation: Pilot and four passengers or internal or external freight
Armament: Provision for armament

Agusta began manufacturing the Bell Model 206 under licence in 1967, and has since completed more than 500 for military and civil use. Production began with the Model 206A, powered by an Allison 250-C18 turboshaft engine, which has a maximum speed of about 150 mph (241 km/h). After several years, production was switched to the 206B JetRanger II version, deliveries of which began in

1972. Users of military versions of the Models 206A and 206B built by Agusta include Austria, Iran, Oman, Saudi Arabia, Spain, Sweden, Turkey and Italy; but only the 206As of the Swedish Navy, designated HPK-6s, were acquired for a specific combat role—anti-submarine and anti-shipping patrol and attack. For these missions the AB 206A carries its weapons (torpedoes, depth bombs, mines, etc) under the fuselage on racks, made possible by the use of a high skid landing gear which has inflatable flotation bags attached to permit landing on water in an emergency.

The civil versions of the AB 206 can accommodate passengers, stretchers or freight. (For full details of the Model 206B JetRanger II, see under Bell.) Corresponding to the Bell Kiowa, Agusta has produced military general-purpose versions of the JetRanger designated AB 206A-1 and AB 206B-1. These are derivatives of the AB 206A and B, differing mainly in having a main rotor of about 2 ft greater diameter, a strengthened airframe, extra doors and provision for armament. Both versions can be used for armed missions, observation and general transport duties.

Agusta-Bell 212 and 212 ASW

Italy

Utility, anti-submarine (212ASW) and attack (212ASW) helicopters, in production and service.

Data: 212ASW
Powered by: One Pratt & Whitney PT6T-6 Turbo Twin Pac coupled turboshaft (derated to 1,290 shp)
Rotor diameter: 48 ft 0 in (14.63 m)
Fuselage length: 46 ft 0 in (14.02 m)
Empty weight: 7,484 lb (3,395 kg)
Gross weight with torpedoes: 11,196 lb (5,079 kg)
Max speed: 122 mph (196 km/h)
Max range: 414 miles (667 km)
Accommodation: Crew of three or four
Armament: Two Mk 44 or Mk 46 homing torpedoes, depth charges or two air-to-surface anti-shipping missiles

Photograph: Agusta-Bell AB-212ASW, with homing torpedo

A twin-engined derivative of the Model 205, the Agusta-Bell 212 is a utility helicopter and can accommodate a pilot plus up to 14 passengers, stretchers, internal or external cargo, rescue or other equipment. Agusta began deliveries of this helicopter in 1971, and by 1975 over 40 had been completed. These are in commercial and military service in Italy and abroad, and production continues.

As a follow-up to the earlier Agusta-Bell 204AS, Agusta has developed a naval version of the 212 for attack missions, as well as for utility and rescue work. Designated 212ASW, this version is similar to the Bell UH-1N (which see) but is strengthened and has deck-mooring equipment. Various

weapons and equipment can be carried by the 212ASW, depending on its mission, and it has been developed to search out and attack both submarines and surface ships. On an ASW mission the helicopter carries a variable-depth sonar and other sophisticated equipment, and the automatic flight control system permits a hands-off flight from the cruise phase to the sonar hover in all weather conditions. For an AWW mission the helicopter uses a long-range search radar, and provision has been made for the carriage of ECM systems. Agusta-Bell 212ASWs are being built for the Italian and Spanish navies and for other countries including Iran and Turkey.

Agusta-Bell Model 47 series   Italy

General-purpose light helicopter, in production and service.

Data: Current versions only; mainly 47J-3B-1 unless otherwise stated
Powered by: One 270 hp Lycoming TVO-435-B1A piston engine
Rotor diameter: 37 ft 1 ½ in (11.32 m)
Fuselage length: 31 ft 7 in (9.63 m)
Empty weight: 1,863 lb (845 kg)
Gross weight: 2,950 lb (1,340 kg)
Max speed: 105 mph (169 km/h)
Range: 210 miles (338 km)
Accommodation: Up to four persons. Approximately 1,000 lb (454 kg) of externally slung freight or stretchers or other equipment
Armament: One Mk 44 torpedo on 47J-3 version

Photograph: Agusta-Bell 47G-4A

In 1952, Agusta received a manufacturing licence from Bell to build Model 47s in Italy. The first aircraft, a Model 47G, flew on May 22, 1954, and production from that time has been continuous. Although only limited production is now being undertaken, well over 1,100 Agusta-Bell 47s have been produced. Current versions in production in Italy are the Models 47G-3B-1, 47G-3B-2, 47G-4A with a 280 hp Lycoming VO-540 engine, 47G-5, 47J-2A, 47J-3 and 47J-3B-1. The last two models are non-standard, having been designed by Agusta for specific Italian requirements. The 47J-3 is basically a standard 47J-2A with a modified main transmission to enable an engine of 260 hp continuous power to be used. Further changes appeared in a version of the 47J-3 developed for the Italian Navy as an ASW helicopter, incorporating special instrumentation for operations at sea

in poor visibility, a high-efficiency rotor brake and provision for carrying a torpedo. The 47J-3B-1 (described above) differs in being developed for high-altitude flying; it has an exhaust-driven supercharger and high-inertia rotor, and the cyclic and collective pitch control systems are servo-controlled.

Bell AH-1 HueyCobra/SeaCobra   USA

Armed helicopter, in production and service.

Data: AH-1J
Powered by: One 1,800 shp Pratt & Whitney (Canada) T400-CP-400 coupled turboshaft (derated to 1,250 shp)
Rotor diameter: 44 ft 0 in (13.41 m)
Fuselage length: 44 ft 7 in (13.59 m)
Gross weight: 10,000 lb (4,535 kg)
Max speed: 207 mph (333 km/h)
Max range: 359 miles (577 km)
Armament: One XM-197 three-barrel 20 mm gun in undernose turret, with 750 rounds. Four attachments under stub-wings for XM-18E1 Minigun pods and 7-tube (XM-157) or 19-tube (XM-159) rocket pods

Photograph: AH-1Q TOW/Cobra

Using the basic transmission, rotor system and power plant of the UH-1 Iroquois, Bell produced in about six months, as a private venture, an armed helicopter for the US Army. The prototype first flew on September 7, 1965, and production aircraft were delivered from June 1967, being deployed in Vietnam the same year. The initial version was designated AH-1G, and had a 1,400 shp Lycoming T53-L-13B turboshaft, derated to 1,100 shp. A fuselage only 38 in (0.97 m) wide made it a difficult target for ground fire, and it was armed originally with an Emerson Electric TAT-102A nose turret housing a six-barrel 7.62 mm Minigun, as well as underwing weapons. Later aircraft replaced the TAT-102A with the XM-28 turret, mounting two Miniguns or two XM-129 40 mm grenade launchers, or one of each. In the early part of 1973, the first of eight pre-production AH-1Q anti-armour HueyCobras was tested by the US Army, with provision for carrying eight Hughes TOW (Tube-launched Optically-tracked Wire-guided) missiles and helmet sight subsystem. AH-1Qs sent to Vietnam achieved impressive results, although the "hot and high" conditions restricted severely the number of TOWs that could be carried. Contracts were placed for conversion of 290 AH-1Gs to AH-1Q standard, and delivery of these began in mid-1975. Further uprating of the design produced the AH-1R and AH-1S. The former has a 1,485 shp Lycoming T53-L-703 engine but cannot carry TOW missiles. The AH-1S also has a T53-L-703, the increased power of which enables it to carry a full complement of eight TOWs under all conditions. The US Army hoped to convert to this standard half of the HueyCobras previously converted into AH-1Qs and all remaining AH-1Gs. The first contract, placed in late 1975, calls for delivery of 44 AH-1Ss during 1977, with an option on 22 more.

Twenty AH-1Gs were delivered to the Spanish Navy for anti-shipping strike operations; the US Marine Corps acquired 38 in 1969, pending delivery of its 69 AH-1J SeaCobras in 1970-71. These are twin-engined, as described in detail at the beginning of this entry, and are being followed by ten improved AH-1Ts, with uprated components for increased payload and performance. Delivery of 202 AH-1Js to Iran began in 1974.

Note: Further illustrations on page 20

Photograph: (top) AH-1J in Iranian Army service   **Photograph:** (above) AH-1G HueyCobra

Bell Model 47

USA

General-purpose helicopter, in service.

Data: Model 47G-3B-2A
Powered by: One 280 hp Lycoming TVO-435-F1A piston engine
Rotor diameter: 37 ft 1 ½ in (11.32 m)
Fuselage length: 31 ft 7 in (9.63 m)
Empty weight: 1,893 lb (858 kg)
Gross weight: 2,950 lb (1,338 kg)
Cruising speed: 84 mph (135 km/h) at 5,000 ft (1,525 m)
Range: 247 miles (397 km) at 6,000 ft (1,830 m)
Accommodation: Pilot and two passengers, 1,000 lb (454 kg) of externally slung freight or stretchers

Photograph: Bell Model 47 Ag-5 agricultural spraying version

Although still in production in Italy (by Agusta, which see), and in developed form in Japan (by Kawasaki, as the KH-4, which see), the Bell 47 was taken off the production line by Bell Helicopter Co. in 1974. This marked the end of 28 years of continuous manufacture by the parent company. The final production models were the Model 47G-3B-2A and the 47G-5A, the latter powered by a 265 hp VO-435-B1A engine. Many hundreds are still in use all over the world.

The design goes back to 1943, when the Bell Aircraft Corporation first flew an experimental helicopter called the Model 30; this was evaluated by the US Army under the designation of XR-12. Two years later, on December 8, 1945, the first flight took place of the prototype Bell Model 47, which had superseded the earlier type. The first Type Approval Certificate for a commercial helicopter, and the first commercial licence, were awarded to the Model 47 by the CAA on March 8, 1946. First orders for production aircraft included 18 for the US Army and ten for the US Navy, since which time large numbers of Model 47s have been produced for military use. The production of major civil variants started with the Model 47B, following the pre-production aircraft with 178 hp Franklin engine and two-seat car-type cabins. The 47B was similar to the pre-production design, although it was also available as the Model 47B-3 with an open cockpit. The next version, which introduced the now-familiar ''goldfish bowl'' type of cabin enclosure, was the Model 47D. An uncovered tailboom and small ventral tail-fin were first seen on the three-seat Model 47D-1. The Model 47E was powered by a 200 hp Franklin 6V4-200-C32 engine and was followed, in 1953, by introduction of the main version, the Bell 47G. The first examples of this variant were powered by a similar engine to the 47E; the subsequent Models 47G-2 to 47G-5 had Lycoming engines of up to 280 hp. The Model 47H was similar to the previous version but with a 200 hp Franklin engine, car-type cabin and a covered tailboom. The four-seat Model 47J Ranger was built in two main versions, the second of which (Model 47J-2) had metal rotor blades and powered controls fitted as standard. Although generally similar to the 47H variant, the 47J and J-2 were powered by a 220 hp Lycoming VO-435 and 260 hp Lycoming VO-540 engine respectively.

Bell Model 205A-1   USA

Commercial utility helicopter, in production and service.

Powered by: One 1,400 shp Lycoming T5313A turboshaft (derated to 1,250 shp)
Rotor diameter: 48 ft 0 in (14.63 m)
Fuselage length: 41 ft 6 in (12.65 m)
Empty weight: 5,197 lb (2,357 kg)
Max gross weight: 10,500 lb (4,763 kg) with external load
Max speed: 127 mph (204 km/h)
Range: 344 miles (553 km) at 8,000 ft (2,440 m)
Accommodation: Pilot and 14 passengers (less in executive configuration) or freight. Alternative layouts enable many roles to be performed

This commercial development of the UH-1H Iroquois was produced to fulfil a number of different roles, including air ambulance (with accommodation for six stretchers and one or two attendants), internal or external freight transport and rescue. Internal freight is loaded through side doors with an opening of 7 ft 8 in × 4 ft 1 in (2.34 m × 1.24 m), and loads of up to 5,000 lb (2,268 kg) can be carried externally.

Superseding the ten-seat Model 204B, the Model 205A-1 has also been built by Agusta of Italy since 1969 and is available in Japan from Fuji.

Photograph: (above) A17 Kiowa of the Australian Army

Photograph: (left) TH-57A SeaRanger
(Details of both types on page 24)

Bell Model 206 JetRanger, OH-58 Kiowa and TH-57 SeaRanger

USA

Military and commercial utility helicopter, light observation helicopter (Kiowa) and military trainer (SeaRanger), in production and service.

Data: Model 206B JetRanger II
Powered by: One 400 shp Allison 250-C20 turboshaft
Rotor diameter: 33 ft 4 in (10.16 m)
Fuselage length: 31 ft 2 in (9.50 m)
Empty weight: 1,455 lb (660 kg)
Gross weight: 3,200 lb (1,451 kg)
Max speed: 140 mph (225 km/h)
Range: 388 miles (624 km) at 5,000 ft (1,525 m)
Accommodation: Pilot and four passengers and 250 lb (113 kg) of baggage. Provision for up to 1,200 lb (545 kg) of externally-slung cargo

Photograph: JetRanger equipped for ambulance duties

The first flight of a Bell Model 206 took place on December 8, 1962. By the beginning of 1976, over 5,000 helicopters of the Model 206 series had been built by Bell and licensed manufacturers (see Agusta-Bell). The Model 206A JetRanger, powered by the 317 shp Allison 250-C18A turboshaft engine, was superseded in production from 1971 by the Model 206B JetRanger II, and conversion kits are available to convert Model 206As into 206Bs. JetRangers have been built for both military and civil use, although only those built by Agusta in Italy for the Swedish Navy have a specific combat role (see Agusta-Bell 206 JetRanger).

On May 23, 1969, the US Army began to receive its first OH-58A Kiowa light observation helicopters, and deployment in Vietnam began that autumn. A total of 2,200 Kiowas had been delivered to that service by the end of 1973. The Kiowa is basically similar to the Model 206A, but has a main rotor diameter of 35 ft 4 in (10.77 m), and revised internal layout and electronics. Between December 16, 1971, and October 1972, 74 similar COH-58As were delivered to Canada, the designation of these later changing to CH-136. In 1971 an agreement was made between Bell and the Australian government under which Model 206B-1 Kiowas would be produced in Australia, following the delivery of 12 from America. The Commonwealth Aircraft Corporation of Australia is assembling the remaining 44 helicopters. The US Navy also acquired a version of the Kiowa, in the form of 40 TH-57A SeaRanger trainers. Other users of the military versions of the Model 206 (not including those produced by Agusta) include the Brazilian Navy, Brunei Army, Jamaica and Sri Lanka.

Bell Model 206L LongRanger   USA

General-purpose commercial helicopter, in production and service.

Powered by: One 420 shp Allison 250-C20B turboshaft
Rotor diameter: 37 ft 0 in (11.28 m)
Fuselage length: 33 ft 3 in (10.13 m)
Empty weight: 1,962 lb (890 kg)
Gross weight: 4,000 lb (1,814 kg)
Max speed: 150 mph (241 km/h)
Range: 385 miles (620 km) at 5,000 ft (1,525 m)
Accommodation: Crew of two plus five passengers, two stretchers and two attendants, or internal or external freight (up to 2,000 lb/907 kg)

Developed from the Model 206B JetRanger II, the LongRanger was announced by Bell in September 1973. It has a longer fuselage than that of the JetRanger and features the Noda-Matic transmission suspension system that was developed by Bell to reduce dramatically the vibration caused by the rotor, thus giving a greater degree of comfort for the passengers. Other improvements over the JetRanger include a revised instrument panel, pedestal and glareshield to improve the forward view, and several external changes to improve maintenance. By careful use of the available space, the 83 cu ft (2.35 m³) cabin can accommodate items with a length of about 8 ft (2.44 m), and loading has been made easier by fitting double doors on one side of the fuselage. These open in such a way as to give a 5 ft (1.52 m) wide opening for cargo loading.

The first flight by a LongRanger took place on September 11, 1974, and production by Bell started in 1975. In the long tradition of co-operation between Bell and Agusta of Italy, the latter company will also produce LongRangers under licence.

Bell Model 212 Twin Two-Twelve   USA

Military and commercial utility helicopter, in production and service.
Data: Twin Two-Twelve
Powered by: One 1,250 shp Pratt & Whitney (Canada) PT6T-3 Turbo Twin Pac, consisting of two coupled PT6 turboshafts
Rotor diameter: 48 ft 2¼ in (14.69 m) with tracking tips
Fuselage length: 42 ft 4¾ in (12.92 m)
Empty weight: 5,549 lb (2,517 kg)
Gross weight: 11,200 lb (5,080 kg)
Max speed: 126 mph (203 km/h)
Range: 273 miles (439 km)
Accommodation: Pilot and 14 passengers or internal or external freight (up to 5,000 lb/2,268 kg externally with commercial version; 3,383 lb/1,534 kg with military version)

Photograph: Model 212 of the Royal Brunei Regiment

Developed originally with Canadian government approval, as a twin-engined version of the Iroquois, many Model 212s have since been built in both military and commercial forms. On September 19, 1969, Bell announced that it had received an order for 50 helicopters for the Canadian Armed Forces, designated CUH-1Ns, with 20 more on option. At the same time it was stated that orders had been received from the US forces. With subsequent orders, these stand at 79 for the US Air Force and 149 for the US Navy/Marine Corps. Deliveries to the US Air Force began in 1970; the Canadian aircraft were delivered between May 1971 and early 1972, later being redesignated CH-135s. The US Navy and Marine Corps also received their first aircraft in 1971, all US examples being designated UH-1Ns. The commercial version of this helicopter is known as the Twin Two-Twelve, and over 250 have been sold. Two Twin Two-Twelves were modified to gain IFR certification, changes including new avionics, a new instrument panel and stabilisation controls. During 1973, twenty IFR-equipped Model 212s were sold to several operators, including the Japanese Maritime Safety Agency, and to a Norway-based company for operations to North Sea oil rigs. Others have since been sold. The Peruvian government is one of the largest operators of the Twin Two-Twelve, with 17. Although based with the Air Force, these helicopters are used in connection with oil exploration and production. (See also Agusta-Bell 212).

Bell Model 214A and 214B   USA

Military and civil utility helicopters, in production and service.

Data: 214B
Powered by: One 2,930 shp Lycoming T5508D turboshaft
Rotor diameter: 50 ft 0 in (15.24 m)
Empty weight (Agusta-built Model 214A): 7,450 lb (3,380 kg)
Gross weight: 16,000 lb (7,257 kg)
Cruising speed: 150 mph (241 km/h)
Accommodation: Pilot and 14 passengers, 7,000 lb (3,175 kg) of externally-slung or 4,000 lb (1,814 kg) of internal freight, agricultural equipment, or 800 US gallons (3,025 litres) of water for fire-fighting

Photograph: Bell Model 214B

Following demonstration flights in Iran by the Model 214A (a development of the prototype Model 214 Huey Plus), the Iranian Imperial Air Force is acquiring 287 examples of this helicopter from the USA. Deliveries started in April 1975, and on the 29th of that month the first helicopter was used to set up records in its class by climbing to a height of 29,760 ft (9,071 m), maintaining a height of 29,760 ft (9,071 m) in horizontal flight, and climbing to 3,000 m, 6,000 m and 9,000 m in record times. Unlike the demonstration aircraft, which was powered by a Lycoming T55-L-7C, production aircraft are fitted with 2,950 shp Lycoming LTC4B-8D engines, the transmission and rotor drive systems evolved on the experimental KingCobra and Noda-Matic vibration-reducing suspension. Range of the Model 214A is said to be about 300 miles (480 km), and it has a maximum take-off weight of 15,000 lb (6,803 kg) with an externally-slung load. The commercial counterpart of the Model 214A was announced by Bell in January 1974 as the Model 214B. Both its main rotor and tail rotor have raked tips, and the main rotor has an advanced hub with elastomeric bearings on the flapping axis. This model became available for purchase in 1975.

The Model 214A is also manufactured in Italy by Agusta. Powered by a similar engine to that of the American-built version, the Agusta-Bell 214A can also accommodate 16 persons and has a maximum take-off weight of 16,000 lb (7,257 kg). Range is said to be 252 miles (405 km).

Bell UH-1 Iroquois   USA

Utility helicopter, in production and service.

Data: UH-1H
Powered by: One 1,400 shp Lycoming T53-L-13 turboshaft
Rotor diameter: 48 ft 0 in (14.63 m)
Fuselage length: 41 ft 10¾ in (12.77 m)
Empty weight: 4,667 lb (2,116 kg)
Gross weight: 9,500 lb (4,309 kg)
Max speed: 127 mph (204 km/h)
Range: 318 miles (511 km)
Accommodation: Pilot and up to 14 troops, or six stretchers and a medical attendant, or 3,880 lb (1,759 kg) of freight

Photograph: UH-1P Iroquois

The first three major versions of the Iroquois belonged to the Bell Model 204 series, with a 44 ft (13.41 m) diameter rotor. First was the HU-1A, with a T53-L-1A engine; deliveries began on June 30, 1959, for utility transport and casualty evacuation, with six seats or two stretchers. It was followed by the HU-1B, accommodating eight passengers or three stretchers and powered by the 960 shp T53-L-5 engine. Its designation was changed to UH-1B after a time, but the nickname of "Huey", resulting from the original HU designation, has continued in use to the present day. Many of this version were built for the US Army and were widely used in Vietnam—some in an armed support role which proved the worth of designing a specialised combat helicopter like the HueyCobra. Variants of the UH-1B have been manufactured by Agusta of Italy (which see) and Fuji of Japan, and have been delivered to the armed forces of Australia, Austria, Ethiopia, the Netherlands, Norway, Saudi Arabia, Spain, Sweden and Turkey. Third Model 204 version was the UH-1C, powered by a 1,100 shp T53-L-11 engine and fitted with a wide-chord rotor.

Soon after deliveries of the original HU-1s began, Bell flew the first of a larger series of Iroquois, covered by the company designation of Model 205. This had the same engine as the UH-1C but was

fitted with a 48 ft (14.63 m) rotor and could accommodate up to 14 passengers. Large orders were placed by the US Army, under the military designation UH-1D, and deliveries started in August 1963. Export customers included Australia, Brazil, Chile and New Zealand, and 352 were manufactured by Dornier for the West German armed forces. For the US Army and New Zealand, the UH-1H superseded the D, with a more powerful T53-L-13 engine (see details at top of this entry). Deliveries to the US Army began in 1967, and very large numbers have since been completed. More than 600, about half the total produced by Bell, were transferred to the South Vietnam Air Force, and 32 were handed to Cambodia. Production of this model is also under way in Taiwan and Japan, with current orders covering 118 UH-1Hs for the Chinese Nationalist Army and about 55 for the Japan Ground Self-Defence Force. UH-1D/H versions have also been produced by Agusta (see Agusta-Bell 205 and 205A-1).

Spin-off variants of the main versions include the UH-1E, a US Marine assault support helicopter developed from the UH-1B; the UH-1F support helicopter of the USAF, ordered first in 1963 with a 1,100 shp General Electric T58-GE-3 engine; the USAF's TH-1F and UH-1P psychological warfare version for use in Vietnam; the US Navy's HH-1K air-sea rescue model, based on the UH-1E, and TH-1L and UH-1L training and utility versions; UH-1M Army helicopters equipped for night sighting of their armament; CH-118s, similar to the UH-1H, for the Canadian Armed Forces; and 30 HH-1H USAF rescue helicopters ordered in 1970.

The 7,000th Model 205 was completed in 1973, since when civil and military production has continued. The twin-engined Model 212 variants, the heavy-lift Bell Model 214A, and civil variants of the Iroquois built by Agusta-Bell are all described separately.

Photograph: (top) US Navy Iroquois in the Antarctic

Photograph: (above) A2 (UH-1H) of RAAF

Boeing Vertol (and Kawasaki) Model 107/ H-46 Sea Knight

USA (and Japan)

Transport, utility and multi-role military helicopter, in production and service.

Data: Kawasaki KV-107/II-2
Powered by: Two 1,250 shp General Electric CT58-110-1 or Ishikawajima-Harima CT58-IHI-110-1 turboshafts
Rotor diameter (each): 50 ft 0 in (15.24 m)
Fuselage length: 44 ft 7 in (13.59 m)
Empty weight: 10,732 lb (4,868 kg)
Gross weight: 19,000 lb (8,618 kg)
Max speed: 168 mph (270 km/h)
Range: 109 miles (175 km) with 6,600 lb (3,000 kg) payload
Accommodation: Crew of two, 25 passengers and 1,500 lb (680 kg) of baggage or freight

Photograph: UH-46D

This helicopter was produced initially by Boeing after it acquired the Vertol Aircraft Corporation, which was responsible for the basic design. The first of three YHC-1A medium transports, built for US Army evaluation, flew on August 27, 1959, powered by two YT58-GE-6 engines. No Army production order followed, but a developed version won a US Marine Corps design competition in February 1961 and was ordered into production as the CH-46A Sea Knight, with 1,250 shp T58-GE-8B engines. The first one flew on October 16, 1962, and more than 600 helicopters of the CH-46 series were eventually ordered. The YHC-1As had meanwhile been redesignated CH-46C. A US Navy model, for ferrying supplies to ships at sea, appeared in 1964 as the UH-46A; 24 were delivered with T58-GE-8B engines, followed by UH-46Ds with T58-GE-10s. Similar engines were fitted in the second Marine Corps version, the CH-46D, which came into being in August 1966. CH-46Fs, with added avionics, came next in 1968, followed in 1974 by the first of some 300 CH-46Es. These are early-model Sea Knights converted to have 1,870

shp T58-GE-16 engines. Exported versions include 18 Model 107-II-9s built for Canada, of which six were to be used by the Air Force as CH-113 Labradors and 12 by the Army as CH-113A Voyageurs before unification of the Canadian Armed Forces. Fourteen Model 107-II-15s, with Bristol Siddeley Gnome H.1200 engines, were supplied to the Royal Swedish Air Force and Navy under the designation HKP-7.

Since 1965, Kawasaki of Japan has held exclusive marketing rights for the 107 Model II, and also has exclusive rights to its manufacture, under the designation KV-107/II. Kawasaki has both civil and military versions available. The KV-107/II-1 is the basic utility version, of which no production has yet been undertaken. The KV-107/II-11 airliner has been produced for several operators, including New York Airways (1), Pan American (2, operated by New York Airways), Air Lift Inc of Japan (2) and three for operation in Thailand. Other civil versions include the KV-107/II-6, the KV-107/II-7 six-to-eleven-seat VIP transport, of which one was purchased by Thailand, and the improved KV-107/IIA-17 long-range version with 1,400 shp CT58-140-1 engines and accommodation for up to 24 passengers, 12 passengers and freight, or stretchers (1 sold to Tokyo Metropolitan Police). Military versions include the KV-107/II-3 mine countermeasures helicopter for the Japanese Navy, of which nine have been purchased, including seven with 1,400 shp engines as KV-107/IIA-3s; KV-107/II-4 transports for the Japanese Army, of which 42 had been delivered by 1976, plus ten with 1,400 shp engines as KV-107/IIA-4s; and the KV-107/II-5 long-range search and rescue version for the Japanese Air Self-Defence Force, of which 22 had been delivered by 1976, including seven with 1,400 shp engines as KV-107/IIA-5s. The Swedish Navy has also bought eight KV-107/II-5s, with additional equipment, and these were fitted with Rolls-Royce Bristol Gnome engines in Sweden after delivery in 1972-74.

Photograph: (top) Kawasaki KV-107/II-4 of the JGSDF, with 'snowshoe' wheel/skis

(above) CH-147 Chinook of the Canadian Armed Forces (see page 32)

Boeing Vertol CH-47 Chinook

USA

Medium transport helicopter, in production and service.

Data: CH-47C
Powered by: Two 3,750 shp Lycoming T55-L-11C turboshafts
Rotor diameter (each): 60 ft 0 in (18.29 m)
Fuselage length: 51 ft 0 in (15.54 m)
Empty weight: 21,464 lb (9,736 kg)
Gross weight: 46,000 lb (20,865 kg)
Max speed: 189 mph (304 km/h)
Mission radius: 115 miles (185 km) at 160 mph (257 km/h) with 11,650 lb (5,285 kg) payload
Accommodation: Crew of two or three and 33-44 equipped troops, 27 paratroops, 24 stretchers and two attendants, or up to 23,212 lb (10,528 kg) of external or 13,212 lb (5,992 kg) of internal freight

Photograph: CH-47B backs into a hillside to unload supplies and equipment while hovering in an area devoid of landing areas

Development of Vertol's Model 114 "battlefield mobility" helicopter began in 1956, and in 1959 the company received a contract for five YHC-1B prototypes, the first of which flew on September 21, 1961. In July 1962 the helicopter's designation was changed to H-47; the prototypes thus became YCH-47As and the initial production aircraft became CH-47As. They were powered originally by 2,200 shp Lycoming T55-L-5 engines, but these were superseded later by 2,650 shp T55-L-7s. Delivery of CH-47As to the US Army began in December 1962; they were used widely in Vietnam by both the Americans and, from 1971, the Vietnamese Air Force. Meanwhile, the first CH-47B had made its maiden flight in October 1966. Powered by 2,850 shp T55-L-7C engines, this version had redesigned rotor blades and minor fuselage modifications; deliveries started in May 1967. On October 14 of that year the first CH-47C (details above) made its initial flight, and production Cs began reaching Vietnam in September 1968. By the end of 1972, more than 550 Chinooks had been despatched to the war zone.

Up to the beginning of 1976, a total of 699 Chinooks had been delivered to the US Army, and it is planned that all remaining CH-47As and Bs will be modified to CH-47C standard. Delivery of eight CH-47Cs to Canada began in September 1974, under the Canadian designation CH-147. Other Boeing-built Chinooks are in service in Australia (12), Spain (7), Thailand (4) and Turkey. In Italy, Meridionali/Agusta has been manufacturing Chinooks under licence since 1970, to fulfil orders placed by the Iranian Imperial Army and Air Force (total of 42) and the Italian Army (26).

Boeing Vertol YUH-61A

USA

Utility transport helicopter, under development.

Data: YUH-61A
Powered by: Two 1,500 shp General Electric T700-GE-700 turboshafts
Rotor diameter: 49 ft 0 in (14.94 m)
Fuselage length: 51 ft 8¾ in (15.77 m)
Empty weight: approximately 9,400 lb (4,264 kg)
Gross weight: 18,700 lb (8,482 kg)
Max cruising speed (Model 179): 184 mph (296 km/h)
Range (Model 179): 598 miles (963 km)
Accommodation: Crew of three plus 11 troops, four stretchers, or freight

On August 30, 1972, the US Department of Defense announced that contracts had been awarded to Boeing Vertol and Sikorsky to construct and test three prototype helicopters each for the US Army's UTTAS (Utility Tactical Transport Aircraft System) programme. Eventual production UTTAS helicopters are to replace Bell UH-1Hs now in service. Boeing Vertol contender is the YUH-61A, the first prototype of which made its maiden flight on November 29, 1974. The second prototype flew on February 19, 1975.

Emphasis placed on keeping to production cost goals, and reliability and ease of maintenance are paramount. The YUH-61A features a simplified hingeless rotor, made of composite materials, which has fewer working parts than previous designs, and is expected to offer improved stability and safety. Many other advanced features are embodied in the helicopter.

A commercial version of the YUH-61A has been developed by Boeing Vertol as the Model 179 (which see).

A further variant is being produced as a contender for the US Navy's Mk III LAMPS programme.

Brantly-Hynes B-2

USA

Light helicopter, in production and service.

Data: B-2B
Powered by: One 180 hp Lycoming IVO-360-A1A piston engine
Rotor diameter: 23 ft 9 in (7.24 m)
Length: 21 ft 9 in (6.62 m)
Empty weight with skids: 1,020 lb (463 kg)
Gross weight: 1,670 lb (757 kg)
Max speed: 100 mph (161 km/h)
Range: 250 miles (400 km)
Accommodation: Two persons and 50 lb (22.7 kg) of baggage

The original B-2 was designed by Mr N. O. Brantly and first flew in 1953. The initial production version was the B-2, powered by a 180 hp Lycoming VO-360-A1A engine. It was followed by the improved B-2A, which featured a redesigned cabin and more comprehensive equipment and led to the major production version, the B-2B. This has a fuel-injected engine and has re-entered production under the present company (Brantly-Hynes, formed in 1975). A further version, the B-2E, was tested as an improved version of the B-2B, with a derated 205 hp Lycoming engine, solid-state instrumentation and better cabin heating, but is not in production. Altogether, about 400 B-2s had been built before manufacture of the B-2B restarted.

Brantly-Hynes Model 305

USA

Light civil helicopter, in production and service.

Powered by: One 305 hp Lycoming IVO-540-A1A piston engine
Rotor diameter: 28 ft 8 in (8.74 m)
Fuselage length: 24 ft 5 in (7.44 m)
Empty weight: 1,800 lb (817 kg)
Gross weight: 2,900 lb (1,315 kg)
Max speed: 120 mph (193 km/h)
Range: 220 miles (354 km) with max fuel and payload
Accommodation: Seating for five persons; compartment for 250 lb (113 kg) of baggage

Basically a scaled-up version of the two-seat Model B-2B, the Model 305 has been put back into production following the formation of Brantly-Hynes Helicopter Inc. It was back in January 1964 that the first prototype made its maiden flight, and the Model 305 received FAA Type Approval in July of the following year. In 1970 all rights in Brantly helicopters were transferred to Brantly Operators Inc, and production was restricted to spare parts for in-service helicopters until Brantly-Hynes Helicopter Inc was founded at the beginning of 1975.

The Model 305 can be fitted with either wheel, skid or twin-float undercarriage.

Photograph: Model 280 Shark

Enstrom Model F-28A and Model 280 Shark   USA

Lightweight civil helicopters, in production and service.

Data: F-28A
Powered by: One 205 hp Lycoming HIO-360-C1A four-cylinder piston engine
Rotor diameter: 32 ft 0 in (9.75 m)
Length: 29 ft 6 in (8.99 m)
Empty weight: 1,450 lb (657 kg)
Gross weight: 2,150 lb (975 kg)
Max speed: 112 mph (180 km/h)
Range: 237 miles (381 km)
Accommodation: Three persons

Photograph: Model F-28A

First major helicopter to be developed by the Enstrom Corporation after its formation in 1959, the F-28 prototype first flew in May 1962. This model entered production and a small number were built before being superseded by the improved F-28A in 1968. From October 1968 to February 1970, the company was owned by the Purex Corporation, but Purex's involvement in Enstrom was subsequently taken over by F. Lee Bailey. Under his management, the F-28A re-entered production, and by the spring of 1975 some 311 examples had been completed. Meanwhile, in 1973, an improved version of the F-28A was flown. Known as the Model 280 Shark, it is similar to the earlier type except for having a more aerodynamically-shaped cabin; dorsal, ventral and small horizontal tail surfaces; and an increased standard fuel capacity which gives it a range of about 315 miles (507 km). It will be certificated eventually with a turbocharged engine.

Fairchild (Hiller) FH-1100

USA

Civil and military utility helicopter, in service.

Powered by: One 317 shp Allison 250-C18 turbo-shaft
Rotor diameter: 35 ft 4 ¾ in (10.79 m)
Fuselage length: 29 ft 9 ½ in (9.08 m)
Gross weight: 2,750 lb (1,247 kg)
Max cruising speed: 127 mph (204 km/h)
Range: 348 miles (560 km)
Accommodation: Five persons

Photograph: FH-1100 of the Argentine Army

On January 26, 1963, the prototype Hiller OH-5A observation helicopter made its first flight. It had been built to take part in a US Army competition which was won subsequently by the Hughes OH-6A Cayuse. Meanwhile, the Hiller company had been taken over by Fairchild in the mid-1960s, and development and manufacture of the OH-5A were continued as a private venture by that company. In its developed form, the OH-5A was redesignated FH-1100 and the first production example was completed on June 3, 1966. It was built for both civil and military use, the first military order coming from the Philippine Air Force which ordered eight. Others still serve with the Argentine Army, Brazilian Navy, and the armed forces of Ecuador and El Salvador.

Hiller UH-12, Model 360 and H-23 Raven   USA

Military and civil light general-purpose helicopter, in service.

Data: Hiller 12E-L3
Powered by: One 305 hp Lycoming VO-540-C2B piston engine
Rotor diameter: 35 ft 5 in (10.80 m)
Fuselage length: 28 ft 6 in (8.69 m)
Empty weight: 1,759 lb (798 kg)
Max gross weight: 3,100 lb (1,405 kg)
Max cruising speed: 90 mph (145 km/h)
Range: 437 miles (703 km) with auxiliary tanks
Accommodation: Pilot and two passengers, and 125 lb (57 kg) of baggage

Photograph: Hiller E4

More than 2,000 helicopters of this series were built for military and civil use and, although production ceased in the 1960s, many are still flying. All are three-seaters except for the four-seat OH-23F and E4.

The first military version was the H-23A, of which 100 were completed for the US Army, 16 for the US Navy (as HTE-1 trainers) and 5 for the US Air Force. The OH-23B version was known originally as the H-23B and featured an uprated engine and dual controls; 273 were built for the US Army and 35 for the US Navy (HTE-2 trainers). The OH-23C, of which 145 were built, was followed by 483 OH-23Ds. Powered by the 250 hp Lycoming VO-435 engine, these preceded the OH-23F, of which 22 were built with Lycoming O-540-9 engines, and the OH-23G. This last version had a similar engine to the OH-23F and 392 were built, including 21 HT. Mk 2 trainers for the Royal Navy and 24 CH-112 Nomads for Canada. In sum, versions of the H-23 were exported to about a dozen different countries. Of the military versions still in use, the most important are the OH-23Ds and OH-23Gs.

The civil variants of the helicopter were built under UH-12 and Model 360 designations and differ considerably throughout the range. The initial version was the Model 12, powered by a 178 hp Franklin 6V4-178-B33 engine. It was followed by the Models 12A, 12B and 12C, powered by 200 hp or 210 hp Franklin engines; the 12C also introduced a "goldfish bowl" cabin enclosure and all-metal rotor blades. The Model 12E was built in two versions, the 12E-L3 and the 12E-SL3 with a 315 hp Lycoming TIVO-540-A2A turbocharged engine. The last variant was the Model E4, a four-seater similar to the military OH-23F, with lengthened fuselage and swept stabilising surfaces. This was produced both as a new aircraft and in the form of a kit to convert the 12E to E4 standard.

Photograph: Model 280U utility version of Model
300, equipped for agricultural spraying

Hughes Model 269 and 300   USA

Military and commercial light helicopter, in production and service.

Data: TH-55A
Powered by: One 180 hp Lycoming HIO-360-B1A piston engine
Rotor diameter: 25 ft 3 ½ in (7.71 m)
Fuselage length: 21 ft 11 ¾ in (6.80 m)
Empty weight: 1,008 lb (457 kg)
Max gross weight: 1,850 lb (839 kg)
Max speed: 86 mph (138 km/h)
Range: 204 miles (328 km)
Accommodation: Two persons in TH-55A; three in Model 300

Photograph: Model 300CQ in Police service

Development of a two-seat light helicopter, known as the Model 269, was undertaken by Hughes Helicopters in 1955. The first prototype made its maiden flight in October 1956 and, following modifications to simplify the design, production began under the designation 269A. Meanwhile, the US Army had successfully evaluated five pre-production examples, under the designation YHO-2HU, for observation and command duties. Deliveries of production aircraft to commercial users began in October 1961, since when the helicopter has been further developed. Current versions are the Model 300, Model 300C and Model 300CQ, and the TH-55A Osage. The first of these is the basic three-seat version, which has been in production since 1964. From mid-1967, production examples have been fitted with a "quiet" tail rotor which lowers the overall noise level of the helicopter by four-fifths, and kits are available to modify earlier Model 300s to this standard. The prototype Model 300C first flew in August 1969,

with a 190 hp Lycoming HIO-360-D1A engine and a rotor of 26 ft 10 in (8.18 m) diameter. These and associated modifications gave an increase in payload of 45% and an increased maximum speed of 105 mph (169 km/h). Licenced production of the Model 300C by BredaNardi of Italy began in 1974. Hughes has also produced a "quiet" version of the Model 300C, known as the Model 300CQ, and existing Model 300Cs can be modified to this standard. By March 1971, no fewer than 1,671 helicopters of the series had been delivered to commercial users.

The designation TH-55A Osage applies to the 792 Model 269As that were delivered to the US Army as primary trainers between 1964 and 1969. Small numbers of similar helicopters have also been purchased for military use in Algeria, Brazil, Colombia, Ghana, Kenya and Nicaragua.

Hughes OH-6 Cayuse and Models 500, 500C and 500M   USA

Military and commercial light helicopter, in production and service.

Data: OH-6A Cayuse
Powered by: One 317 shp Allison T63-A-5A turboshaft (derated to 252.5 shp)
Rotor diameter: 26 ft 4 in (8.03 m)
Fuselage length: 23 ft 0 in (7.01 m)
Empty weight: 1,229 lb (557 kg)
Gross weight: 2,400 lb (1,090 kg)
Max speed: 150 mph (241 km/h)
Range: 380 miles (611 km) at 5,000 ft (1,525 m)
Accommodation: Crew of two and up to four troops or freight
Armament: Provision for carrying an XM-27 7.62 mm machine-gun or an XM-75 grenade launcher

Photograph: (above) OH-6A Cayuse, with multi-barrel machine-gun in fuselage-side pack

The OH-6A Cayuse is a light observation helicopter of the US Army. Five prototypes were built originally for evaluation against similar types from Bell and Hiller, and the first of these flew on February 27, 1963. The Hughes helicopter was chosen by the Army, and by August 1970 that service had received all of the 1,434 OH-6As ordered. In April 1971 Hughes divulged the existence of an experimental version of the Cayuse and claimed it to be the quietest helicopter in the world. Known as "the Quiet One", it had a five-blade (instead of four-blade) main rotor, a four-blade (instead of two-blade) tail rotor, an engine exhaust muffler and a completely blanketed engine assembly. Further versions of the Cayuse are the OH-6C, which has flown at 200 mph (322 km/h) while powered by a 400 hp Allison 250-C20 turboshaft, and the proposed OH-6D Advanced

Scout Helicopter. From April 1968, the military export version, designated Model 500M, has been delivered to several foreign armed forces, including the Spanish Navy (for anti-submarine duties, with provision for MAD and two Mk 44 torpedoes), Mexico, the Philippines, Colombia, Denmark and Argentina. Others are built by Kawasaki of Japan (97 delivered as OH-6Js for JGSDF, 3 for the JMSDF and 34 for civil operators by early 1976), by BredaNardi of Italy (for the Italian Army; an anti-submarine version has also been produced), and by RACA of Argentina.

The Models 500 and 500C are commercial versions of the helicopter. The former is powered (like the Model 500M) by a 317 shp Allison 250-C18A (civil version of the T63-A-5A), derated to 278 shp. Payload is normally a pilot and four passengers or internal or external freight, but up to seven persons can be carried. Optional equipment includes dual controls, cargo hook, hoist and stretcher kit. The Model 500C differs in having a 400 shp Allison 250-C20 turboshaft (derated to 278 shp) for hot-day/high-altitude operations. Civil variants of the Hughes Model 500 assembled in Japan by Kawasaki are known as Model 369HSs.

Photograph: (top right) Hughes 500M equipped for anti-submarine duties with the Spanish Navy

Photograph: (below) Hughes 500D in flying-crane role (see page 44 for details)

Hughes Model 500D

USA

Light commercial helicopter, in production and service.

Powered by: One 420 shp Allison 250-C20B turboshaft
Rotor diameter: 26 ft 5 in (8.05 m)
Fuselage length: 23 ft 0 in (7.01 m)
Empty weight: 1,320 lb (598 kg)
Gross weight: 3,000 lb (1,360 kg)
Max speed: 175 mph (281 km/h)
Range: 369 miles (594 km) at 5,000 ft (1,525 m)
Accommodation: Pilot and four or six passengers

Generally similar to the Model 500C in dimensions and appearance, the prototype 500D first flew in August 1974. It differs from the Model 500C mainly in having a more powerful engine, strengthened transmission, larger-diameter five-blade rotor, teetering tail rotor, and a T-tail, which gives the helicopter better stability in both high- and low-speed flight, and also improves its handling characteristics during exceptional flying modes. It was hoped that the Model 500D would be certificated in both Normal and Utility categories by early 1976.

The pilot and two passengers are accommodated on a front bench seat, leaving the rear section of the cabin free for up to four more passengers. A baggage compartment is provided under the seats. Optional equipment includes a 2,000 lb (907 kg) capacity cargo sling and a hoist for rescue duties.

Kaman H-2 Seasprite   USA

Ship-based anti-submarine, missile defence and utility helicopter, in service.

Data: SH-2F
Powered by: Two 1,350 shp General Electric T58-GE-8F turboshafts
Rotor diameter: 44 ft 0 in (13.41 m)
Length, nose and blades folded: 38 ft 4 in (11.68 m)
Empty weight: 7,040 lb (3,193 kg)
Gross weight: 12,800 lb (5,805 kg)
Max speed: 165 mph (265 km/h)
Range: 422 miles (679 km)
Accommodation: Crew of three
Armament: Mk 44 or Mk 46 homing torpedoes can be carried on auxiliary fuel tank attachments

Photograph: (above) YSH-2E with experimental radar
Photograph: (left) SH-2F, showing sonobuoy tubes and homing torpedo on port side

The prototype Seasprite flew for the first time on July 2, 1959, powered by a single 1,250 shp T58-GE-8B engine. The initial production version for the US Navy was the generally similar UH-2A all-weather utility helicopter, of which 88 were built, entering service from mid-December 1962. They were followed in August 1963 by the first of 102 UH-2Bs, with electronics for VFR operation only. However, all UH-2As and Bs were subsequently re-engined with two T58-GE-8Fs and redesignated UH-2C. They began to be deployed by the Navy in the latter part of 1967, and all subsequent versions of the Seasprite have been converted UH-2Cs. First of them was the NUH-2C, a single aircraft that was modified originally to carry Sparrow III missiles and associated equipment, to examine the feasibility of using Seasprites as missile launch platforms. The same aircraft was tested in 1975 as the NHH-2D, to evaluate methods of landing helicopters on small ship platforms under the Navy's Hauldown/Secure/Traverse programme. Six HH-2Cs were produced for search and rescue duties in Southeast Asia, with added armament, armour plating, four-blade tail rotor, paired main wheels and increased gross weight. Next came 67 HH-2Ds, similar to HH-2Cs but without the armament and armour. In 1971, two of the HH-2Ds were modified for testing in an anti-ship missile defence (ASMD) role under the Navy's LAMPS (Light Airborne Multi-Purpose System) programme. They were fitted with experimental undernose radar and were evaluated on board the USS *Fox*. Two others became testbeds for anti-submarine warfare (ASW) equipment and were evaluated on the USS *Wainwright* and USS *Belknap*. As a result of these tests, it was decided to convert 20 HH-2D Seasprites to SH-2D LAMPS configuration, with Canadian Marconi LN 66 high-power surface search radar in a chin housing, towed magnetic anomaly detector (MAD), active or passive sonobuoys, flare/smoke markers, torpedoes and other equipment. The first SH-2D flew on March 16, 1971, and deployment began in December of the same year. A further two HH-2Ds have since been modified, this time as YSH-2Es, and are being used to develop an advanced Mk III version of LAMPS. Meanwhile, all remaining UH-2Cs and HH-2Ds had been converted to the latest SH-2F standard by the end of 1975, and it is intended that the SH-2Ds will follow. The SH-2F has a new high-performance, vibration-free rotor, improved LN 66HP radar, a repositioned tailwheel midway along the rear fuselage and other modifications. It is expected to be qualified eventually at a gross weight of 13,300 lb (6,033 kg).

Kamov Ka-25 (NATO code-name: Hormone)　　　　USSR

Anti-submarine and general-purpose helicopter, in service.

Data: based on the Ka-25K
Powered by: Two 900 shp Glushenkov GTD-3 turboshafts
Rotor diameter: 51 ft 8 in (15.74 m)
Length: 32 ft 0 in (9.75 m)
Gross weight: 16,100 lb (7,300 kg)
Max speed: 137 mph (220 km/h)
Accommodation: Probably crew of three or four. Twelve passengers in transport version
Armament: Internal weapons bay in cabin undersurface for stores, including torpedoes and nuclear depth charges

The Ka-25 was first seen as a prototype during a Soviet Aviation Day display, near Moscow, on July 9, 1961. Given the NATO code-name "Harp", this prototype carried two dummy air-to-surface missiles, on outriggers on each side of the cabin. Production aircraft, code-named "Hormone", do not appear to have such an installation. In an anti-submarine configuration, the Ka-25 serves on the Soviet Navy's helicopter carriers *Moskva* and *Leningrad,* each of which carries about 20 helicopters, and on *Kara* and *Kresta* class cruisers. Equipment includes an undernose search radar, two versions of which seem to exist, dipping sonar, towed magnetic anomaly detector, an electro-optical sensor and inflatable pontoons around each wheel of the undercarriage. In a transport role, the Ka-25 can accommodate twelve passengers on folding seats.

Kamov Ka-25K (NATO code-name: Hormone)　　　USSR

Flying-crane and general-purpose helicopter.

Powered by: Two 900 shp Glushenkov GTD-3 turboshafts
Rotor diameter: 51 ft 8 in (15.74 m)
Length: 32 ft 3 in (9.83 m)
Empty weight: 9,700 lb (4,400 kg)
Max payload: 4,400 lb (2,000 kg)
Gross weight: 16,100 lb (7,300 kg)
Max speed: 137 mph (220 km/h)
Range: over 405 miles (650 km)
Accommodation: Crew of two and twelve passengers or freight

The Ka-25K is the commercial counterpart of the Ka-25 and was first seen at the 1967 Paris Air Show. It differs from the military version in being a few inches longer and has an undernose control gondola instead of the radome. Although the Ka-25K is a general-purpose helicopter, its main role is that of a flying crane, which explains the fixed gondola. One of the crew sits in this, facing the rear of the helicopter, during ground handling of the externally-slung freight and, with the aid of dual controls in the gondola, controls the helicopter while it is hovering. This allows the "lower deck" pilot to see what is happening below, and to make any necessary hovering flight corrections during this operation. Cargo can also be carried internally, and the cabin can be arranged alternatively to accommodate twelve persons on folding seats.

Kamov Ka-26 (NATO code-name: Hoodlum)　　　USSR

Military and civil light general-purpose helicopter, in production and service.

Powered by: Two 325 hp M-14V-26 radial piston engines
Rotor diameter: 42 ft 8 in (13.00 m) each
Fuselage length: 25 ft 5 in (7.75 m)
Empty weight: 4,300 lb (1,950 kg)
Gross weight: 7,165 lb (3,250 kg)
Max speed: 105 mph (170 km/h)
Range: 248 miles (400 km) with 7 passengers and reserves
Accommodation: Crew of one or two, plus six passengers, etc (see below)

Photograph: (above) Geophysical survey version of Ka-26

More widely used as a civil rather than military helicopter, the Ka-26 first flew in 1965. Special features include contra-rotating co-axial three-blade rotors, podded engines mounted on small stub wings, plastics tailbooms fitted with horizontal and vertical tail surfaces (the twin fins and rudders being toed inwards at 15º), and a detachable fuselage section aft of the flight deck. In the space provided for the detachable fuselage section can be positioned interchangeable pods for passengers and freight, agricultural chemicals and spraying equipment; or the helicopter can be flown with a platform for a ton of cargo, or without any pod or platform but fitted with a cargo hook.

Civil versions of the Ka-26 are in service in the USSR and in Bulgaria, East Germany, West Germany, Hungary, Romania and Sweden. They are used for a variety of roles, in addition to those mentioned above, including air ambulance (with two stretchers, two sitting casualties and an attendant), fire-fighting (carrying six men and fire-fighting equipment), dual-control training, pipeline construction, geophysical survey (with an electromagnetic pulse generator in the cabin and carrying a hoop antenna), aerial survey, fish-spotting (operating from a small vessel), ice-breaking survey and rescue. In military form, the Ka-26 is in service with the air forces of the USSR, Sri Lanka and Hungary.

Photograph: (above) Agricultural Ka-26 with chemical dust hopper

Photograph: Ka-26 with passenger cabin

Kawasaki KH-4

Japan

General-purpose helicopter, in service.

Powered by: One 270 hp Lycoming TVO-435-D1A piston engine
Rotor diameter: 37 ft 1 ½ in (11.32 m)
Fuselage length: 32 ft 7 ¼ in (9.93 m)
Empty weight: 1,890 lb (857 kg)
Gross weight: 2,850 lb (1,292 kg)
Max speed: 105 mph (169 km/h)
Range: 214 miles (345 km)
Accommodation: Pilot and three passengers, stretchers or freight

Kawasaki has manufactured the Bell Model 47 under licence since 1953, producing a total of about 240 examples, mostly Model 47G-2s. It also developed from the Bell Model 47G-3B a four-seat helicopter known as the KH-4. In addition to the changed cabin configuration, this has a modified control system, improved instrument layout and extra fuel. The prototype flew for the first time in August 1962. By February 1975, a total of 158 KH-4s had been purchased for civil operation and a further 53 had been delivered for military service with the Japan Ground Self-Defence Force (19) and the armed forces of Korea (5), the Philippines (1) and Thailand (28). As alternatives to the basic four-seat passenger configuration, kits can be provided to equip the KH-4 for agricultural work, stretcher carrying and external freight transportation. Other optional equipment includes an auxiliary fuel tank, pontoons and a loudspeaker.

MBB BO 105   Germany

Utility helicopter, in production and service.

Powered by: Two 400 shp Allison 250-C20 turboshafts
Rotor diameter: 32 ft 2¾ in (9.82 m)
Length: 28 ft 0½ in (8.55 m)
Empty weight: 2,469 lb (1,120 kg)
Gross weight: 5,070 lb (2,300 kg)
Max speed: 167 mph (270 km/h)
Range: 408 miles (656 km) with standard fuel
Accommodation: Pilot and four passengers and/or freight or two stretchers
Armament: Provision for six Hot anti-tank missiles, carried on outriggers, or other stores on military version

Photograph: (above) BO 105 fitted with rescue hoist and inflatable pontoons

Following ground tests of a rigid unarticulated rotor, with only feathering hinges, construction of three prototype BO 105s was initiated in 1964. The first was flown with two 317 shp Allison 250-C18 turboshaft engines and a conventional rotor; but the second and third prototypes — the third powered by MAN-Turbo 6022 engines — were fitted with the new rigid rotor. They made their first flights on February 16, 1967, and December 20, 1967, respectively. There followed two pre-production aircraft, the second of which was later re-engined with more powerful Allison 250-C20 turboshafts, with which it flew on January 11, 1971.

The standard production version of the helicopter is the BO 105C, which has been fitted with 250-C20 engines since 1973, and "droop-snoot" rotor blades, designed by MBB, since 1970. By the beginning of 1975, about 185 BO 105s had been built, in both civil and military versions, many of them for export. Further orders have been placed, and it is thought likely that about 300 will be ordered for the German Army. A modified version of the helicopter, designated BO 105D, has been delivered to Great Britain. This is capable of being operated in Instrument Meteorological Conditions, so permitting night operations to and from oil rig platforms at sea.

Under a licence granted by MBB, the Philippine Aerospace Development Corporation is manufacturing 33 BO 105Cs, the first of which was completed in August 1974. MBB's US agents, Boeing Vertol, are marketing a "stretched" version known as the Executaire (which see).

Photograph: (above) BO 105 equipped with six Hot missile launchers and stabilised sight

51

Mil Mi-4 (NATO code-name: Hound)   USSR

Military transport, ASW and general-purpose helicopter; and civil general-purpose and agricultural helicopter, in service.

Data: Mi-4P civil transport
Powered by: One 1,700 shp Shvetsov ASh-82V piston engine
Rotor diameter: 68 ft 11 in (21.00 m)
Fuselage length: 55 ft 1 in (16.80 m)
Max gross weight: 17,200 lb (7,800 kg)
Max speed: 130 mph (210 km/h) at 5,000 ft (1,500 m)
Range: 155 miles (250 km) with 11 passengers and 220 lb (100 kg) of baggage
Accommodation: Crew of two plus 8-11 passengers or 3,525 lb (1,600 kg) of freight. Eight stretchers and a medical attendant can be carried in ambulance version; Mi-4S agricultural version carries up to 352 Imp gallons (1,600 litres) of chemicals and equipment

Photograph: Anti-submarine version of Mi-4

First flown in 1952, the Mi-4 entered service during the following year. Many thousands were built, in both civil and military configurations, for operation in the USSR and for export. The Mi-4 was the second Soviet-designed helicopter to go into quantity production, after the small Mi-1, and bears a close resemblance to the Sikorsky S-55, which preceded it into service. However, the Mi-4 has important differences compared with the S-55, including clamshell rear loading doors and a fairing under the front fuselage in the military versions for a navigator or observer. A machine-gun is carried in this position when the Mi-4 is used on army support duties, and this helicopter can also carry air-to-surface rockets. The anti-submarine version has an undernose search radar, a MAD towed "bird" and racks for flares, markers or sonobuoys. As a military transport, the Mi-4 can accommodate up to 14 troops or freight, the latter including a GAZ-69 command truck or a 76 mm anti-tank gun. Military Mi-4s serve with the armed forces of many countries, including Afghanistan, Albania, Algeria, Bulgaria, Cambodia, China, Cuba, Czechoslovakia, Egypt, Finland, East Germany, Hungary, India, Indonesia, Iraq, North Korea, Mali, Mongolia, Poland, Romania, Somalia, Syria, USSR, Vietnam, Yemen and Yugoslavia.

Civil variants of the Mi-4 include the standard freighter version, the Mi-4P passenger or ambulance version, and the agricultural Mi-4S.

Mil Mi-6 (NATO code-name: Hook)   USSR

Heavy transport and military assault helicopter, in production and service.

Powered by: Two 5,500 shp Soloviev D-25V (TV-2BM) turboshafts
Rotor diameter: 114 ft 10 in (35.00 m)
Fuselage length: 108 ft 10 ½ in (33.18 m)
Empty weight: 60,055 lb (27,240 kg)
Max gross weight: 93,700 lb (42,500 kg)
Max speed: 186 mph (300 km/h)
Range: 652 miles (1,050 km) with 9,480 lb (4,300 kg) payload
Accommodation: Crew of five and 65 passengers, 41 stretchers and two attendants, 26,450 lb (12,000 kg) of internal or 19,840 lb (9,000 kg) of externally-slung freight, or other equipment, including several tons of water in tanks for fire-fighting
Armament: Provision for a gun in the nose of some aircraft

Designed for both civil and military use, the Mi-6 was first exhibited in 1957. It was then the largest helicopter in the world and, assuming that the Mil V-12 (Mi-12) is not yet fully operational in Russia, remains the largest in service in 1976. It was also the first turbine-powered helicopter to go into series production in the USSR, initial Mi-6s off the assembly line being delivered as assault transports for the Soviet Air Force. Development of the helicopter is thought to have been carried out with five prototypes, which have been followed by 30 pre-production and more than 500 production Mi-6s. Those of the Soviet Air Force have been demonstrated often in their tactical assault role, carrying troops, supplies and complete artillery missile systems. Others are operated by Aeroflot for passenger and freight services in remote areas, and for the varied roles listed above, and have also been supplied to the air forces of Bulgaria, Egypt, Iraq, Indonesia and Vietnam.

The Mi-6 has clamshell rear doors and folding ramps for the loading of freight and vehicles, and is fitted with small shoulder-mounted wings to offset the rotor in flight. These wings are normally removed when the helicopter operates as a flying crane. (A purpose-built flying crane version of the Mi-6 is the Mi-10, which see.)

Photograph: Troops disembarking from a hovering Mi-8

Mil Mi-8 (NATO code-name: Hip)   USSR

General-purpose, assault and commercial transport helicopter, in production and service.

Powered by: Two 1,500 shp Isotov TV2-117A turboshafts
Rotor diameter: 69 ft 10 ¼ in (21.29 m)
Fuselage length: 60 ft 0 ¾ in (18.31 m)
Empty weight (passenger version): 16,007 lb (7,261 kg)
Max gross weight: 26,455 lb (12,000 kg)
Max speed: 161 mph (260 km/h)
Range (cargo version at normal AUW): 298 miles (480 km)
Accommodation: Crew of two or three and 28-32 passengers, 12 stretchers and a medical attendant, 8,820 lb (4,000 kg) of internal freight or 6,614 lb (3,000 kg) of externally-slung freight in transport versions
Armament: Twin-rack for external stores on outrigger on each side of cabin

Photograph: Commercial Mi-8 in Aeroflot service

Designed as a replacement for the Mi-4, the Mi-8 is able to use Mi-4 rotor blades and secondary gearboxes in an emergency. More than 1,000 had been constructed by mid-1974, just under a third of which were exported. Mi-8s are available in both military and civil versions, and serve with the air forces of Afghanistan, Bangladesh, Bulgaria, Czechoslovakia, Egypt, Ethiopia, Finland, East Germany, Hungary, India, Iraq, Pakistan, Peru, Poland, Romania, Somalia, South Yemen, Sudan, Syria, the USSR and Yugoslavia. The first prototype made its public debut at the Soviet Aviation Dav display in 1961, powered by a single 2,700 shp . oloviev engine, driving a four-blade rotor. All subsequent aircraft have had two Isotov engines side-by-side above the cabin. The first twin-engined Mi-8 made its maiden flight on September 17, 1962, and the original four-blade rotor was replaced by a five-blade type in 1964.

Three civil versions of the Mi-8 are available: the standard Mi-8, seating up to 32 passengers; the Mi-8T utility version, used mostly for freight carrying although it can accommodate up to 24 passengers; and the Mi-8 Salon with executive seating for eleven passengers. Mi-8s in service with Aeroflot are also used for ambulance, rescue, supply carrying, ice patrol and reconnaissance duties, the latter in the Antarctic.

A version of the Mi-8 equipped with floats is reported to be under evaluation in the USSR, designated Mil V-14.

Mil Mi-10 (NATO code-name: Harke)　　　　　USSR

Heavy flying-crane and general-purpose helicopter, in service.

Powered by: Two 5,500 shp Soloviev D-25V turboshafts
Rotor diameter: 114 ft 10 in (35.00 m)
Fuselage length: 107 ft 9¾ in (32.86 m)
Empty weight: 60,185 lb (27,300 kg)
Gross weight: 96,340 lb (43,700 kg)
Max speed: 124 mph (200 km/h)
Range: 155 miles (250 km) with a 12,000 kg load on platform
Accommodation: Crew of three plus up to 28 passengers or/and freight (the latter carried internally, externally on a platform or locked into place, or by sling gear)

Photograph: Mi-10 without external load

Developed from the Mil Mi-6, the Mi-10 first flew in 1960. Although it is able to carry internal freight or passengers, and to perform more general duties such as rescue, its main function is to operate as a flying crane. Compared with the Mi-6, it has a much shallower fuselage, no shoulder-mounted wings, and tall wide-track undercarriage legs, with a ground clearance of 12 ft 3½ in (3.75 m) and a track of 22 ft 8½ in (6.92 m) on the main wheels. This enables the Mi-10 to position itself over a load to be carried, without first having to take off. Cargoes can be pre-loaded on a specially-designed wheeled platform, which is locked into position and can weigh up to 15,000 kg; or can be attached to the same hydraulic grips without a platform, making it possible for items over 65 ft long, 32 ft wide and 10 ft high (20 m × 10 m × 3.1 m) to be lifted and locked in place in under 2 minutes. Unlike the Mi-10K version (which see), the Mi-10's observation gondola, originally fitted under the nose of the helicopter, has been superseded by a TV monitoring system in which cameras, placed at the rear of the fuselage and at the sling-load hatch, display the area below the fuselage.

Mil Mi-10s are in service with the Soviet armed forces and with Aeroflot, and the type is offered for export.

Mil Mi-10K

USSR

Heavy flying-crane helicopter, in service.

Powered by: Two 5,500 shp Soloviev D-25V turboshafts
Rotor diameter: 114 ft 10 in (35.00 m)
Fuselage length: 107 ft 9¾ in (32.86 m)
Empty weight: 54,410 lb (24,680 kg)
Gross weight with slung load: 83,776 lb (38,000 kg)
Max cruising speed with slung load: 125 mph (202 km/h)
Ferry range: 494 miles (795 km) with auxiliary fuel
Accommodation: Crew of two (minimum) plus up to 28 passengers and/or freight

Photograph: Mi-10K lifting a sevon-ton assembly to the top of an 820 ft power station chimney

Developed from the Mi-10, the Mi-10K was first seen on March 26, 1966, at Moscow. It differs from the earlier model in having an overall height of only 25 ft 7 in (7.80 m) — compared with 32 ft 2 in (9.80 m) for the Mi-10 — because of its shorter under-carriage legs, and has an undernose gondola. A further change will be replacement of the present engines with 6,500 shp Soloviev D-25VFs at a later date. This is expected to raise the maximum possible slung payload from 24,250 lb (11,000 kg) to 30,865 lb (14,000 kg).

As on the smaller Kamov Ka-25K, the undernose gondola enables one of the crew to control the hovering flight of the helicopter, via flight controls and a rearward-facing seat, while directly observing the handling of the cargo below the fuselage, which would be out of sight from the conventional flight deck.

During May 1965, an Mi-10K set up five official records, starting with a Class E-1 record for climbing to an altitude of 23,461 ft (7,151 m) with a 5,000 kg payload. The other four records were all set during a single flight in which, on May 28, the helicopter lifted a 55,347 lb (25,105 kg) payload to an altitude of 9,318 ft (2,840 m). None still stands.

Mil Mi-24 (NATO code-name: Hind)　　　　　　USSR

Armed assault helicopter, in production and service.

Data: "Hind-A"
Powered by: Two turboshaft engines of approximately 1,500 shp each
Rotor diameter (estimated): 55 ft 9 in (17.00 m)
Length (estimated): 55 ft 9 in (17.00 m)
Height (estimated): 14 ft 0 in (4.25 m)
Accommodation: Crew of two and about eight fully-equipped troops
Armament: One 12.7 mm flexibly-mounted machine-gun in nose. Attachments on wingtips for four "Swatter" anti-tank missiles, and under wings for four rocket pods, each containing thirty-two 57 mm rockets, or other stores.

Known to have been in existence since 1972, the Mi-24 is operational with the Soviet armed forces, including two units of approximately squadron strength stationed in East Germany. It was believed originally to be a development of the Mi-8, but the Mi-24 is now generally accepted as a new design, smaller than the Mi-8, with a new wide-chord main rotor and engines of smaller size than those of the older aircraft, although estimated to be of roughly equal power. Only the tail rotor appears to be the same on both helicopters. Other notable design features include tapered wings with 20° of incidence, a sweptback fin/tail rotor pylon that is "twisted" a few degrees to port, a main cabin large enough to accommodate eight troops, and a fully retractable wheeled undercarriage.

The first version of the Mi-24 was code-named "Hind-B" and had wings without anhedral or dihedral. Each wing had only two weapon attachment points, and it is believed that few examples of this version were built. The further developed major production version is the "Hind-A", each wing of which has pronounced anhedral and three stores attachment points, the outermost point carrying two rails for air-to-surface missiles.

Mil V-12 (Mi-12) (NATO code-name: Homer)   USSR

Heavy general-purpose helicopter, in production and service.

Powered by: Four 6,500 shp Soloviev D-25VF turboshafts
Rotor diameter: 114 ft 10 in (35.00 m) each
Fuselage length: 121 ft 4 ½ in (37.00 m)
Gross weight: 231,500 lb (105,000 kg)
Max speed: 161 mph (260 km/h)
Range: 310 miles (500 km) with 78,000 lb (35,400 kg) payload
Accommodation: Crew of six plus 50 passengers and freight

In the Soviet Union, work began in 1965 on this massive transport helicopter. It was designed to a specification calling for a VTOL aircraft that would carry payloads, including missiles, compatible with those carried by the giant Antonov An-22 Antheus fixed-wing transport. Its existence was revealed officially in March 1969, after the prototype had set up several payload-to-height records. Later in the same year it beat its own records by reaching a height of 7,398 ft (2,255 m) with an 88,636 lb (40,204.5 kg) payload. However, it was also in 1969 that the prototype crashed through engine failure. Production of the type was expected to begin in 1971, at which time two further prototypes were flying.

The V-12 is powered by four engines, arranged as two engine-and-rotor packages which are mounted at the ends of the fixed, high-mounted, inversely-tapering wings. Each of these packages is generally similar to that used on the Mil Mi-10. Loading of the freight hold is carried out through rear clamshell-type doors, via a loading ramp. An electrically-operated movable crane slides along rails in the roof of the cabin and can lift up to 22,000 lb (10,000 kg) of freight at one time. The seats provided for troops or work parties fold upward along the cabin walls when not in use.

Production V-12s are expected to be operated by Aeroflot, as well as by the Soviet armed forces. They will be used principally for supporting oil and gas explorations; transporting freight, vehicles and geophysical survey equipment in remote areas of the Soviet Union. Normal payloads for the V-12 are 55,000 lb (25,000 kg) in VTOL and 66,000 lb (30,000 kg) in STOL operations.

Sikorsky S-55, H-19 Chickasaw, and Westland Whirlwind

USA/Great Britain

Commercial and military general-purpose helicopters, in service.

Data: H-19 Chickasaw (R-1300 engined versions)
Powered by: One 800 hp Wright R-1300-3 piston engine (UH-19B, UH-19D, CH-19E and UH-19F). One 600 hp Pratt & Whitney R-1340 engine (UH-19C)
Rotor diameter: 53 ft 0 in (16.15 m)
Fuselage length: 42 ft 3 in (12.88 m)
Gross weight: 7,900 lb (3,583 kg)
Max speed: 112 mph (180 km/h)
Range: 360 miles (580 km)
Accommodation: Crew of two and ten troops, six stretchers or freight

Photograph: Aviation Specialties S-55T conversion

The H-19 is the military equivalent of the commercial S-55. Sikorsky built 1,281, most of which went for military service in America. These included the USAF's UH-19B, the US Army's UH-19C and UH-19D, the US Marine Corps' CH-19E and the US Navy's UH-19F. The armed forces of many other countries were supplied with versions of the S-55 and H-19 for utility transport, air ambulance, and search and rescue, including those of Argentina, Brazil, Dominican Republic, Ghana, Greece, Guatemala, Honduras, Japan, South Korea, Spain, Taiwan, Thailand, Turkey and Venezuela. Other S-55s and H-19s were licence-built by Mitsubishi of Japan and by Westland of the UK, the latter as Whirlwinds. The Whirlwind was built in three forms by Westland (Series 1-3), the first being a licence-built S-55. In its Series 2 form, the Whirlwind underwent considerable development, including use of the 750 hp Alvis Leonides Major engine which improved the performance. The Series 3 version changed again to the 1,050 hp Rolls-Royce Bristol Gnome H.1000 turboshaft engine. More than 400 Series 1 and 2 Whirlwinds were built for civil and military use, including many for the RAF and Royal Navy. A few remain in RAF service as HAR Mk 10s for SAR, these being Series 3 conversions of earlier piston-engined models. Whirlwinds of all three versions were exported to the Brazilian Navy, Cuba, Ghana, Iran, Jordon, Nigeria, Qatar and Yugoslavia. In January 1971, Aviation Specialties of the USA obtained certification for a turbine-powered version of the S-55, in the Transport Category. This version of the helicopter, known as the S-55T, is basically an S-55 with the original Wright or Pratt & Whitney piston engine replaced by an 840 shp Garrett-AiResearch TSE331-3U-303 turboshaft (derated to 650 shp). Other modifications found in the S-55T include transfer of a number of mechanical and electronic components from the tailboom to the forward compartment to ease maintenance. The gross weight of this version is 7,200 lb (3,265 kg), and both the maximum speed and range are marginally improved. By February 1975, 32 S-55s had been converted to S-55Ts and were being operated in Alaska, Canada, Chile, the USA and in Europe. Over 100 such conversions are expected to be carried out eventually.

Photograph: Whirlwind HAR Mk 10

Sikorsky S-58 and S-58T

Civil transport and military general-purpose and anti-submarine helicopter, in service.

Data: S-58T Mk II
Powered by: One 1,875 shp Pratt & Whitney (Canada) PT6T-6 Twin-Pac twin-turboshaft engine
Rotor diameter: 56 ft 0 in (17.07 m)
Fuselage length: 47 ft 3 in (14.40 m)
Empty weight: 8,354 lb (3,789 kg)
Gross weight: 13,000 lb (5,896 kg)
Max speed: 138 mph (222 km/h)
Range: 278 miles (447 km) with 283 US gallons (1,071 litres) of fuel
Accommodation: Crew of two plus 10-16 passengers or freight

Photograph: S-58T conversion

Between 1954 and January 1970, no fewer than 1,821 Sikorsky S-58s were built, mostly for military service but a number also for civil operators. In mid-1952, the US Navy had placed a contract with Sikorsky for an anti-submarine helicopter. This prototype, designated XHSS-1, first flew on March 8, 1954, and subsequent versions produced for the Navy included the SH-34G Seabat, the improved SH-34J with automatic stabilisation equipment, and the LH-34D, which was equipped for cold-weather operation. Later, the Navy versions were used as utility helicopters redesignated UH-34G and UH-34J. The US Marine Corps operated the S-58 in UH-34D Seahorse, UH-34E and VH-34D versions for utility, amphibious utility and VIP transport respectively. Six HH-34Fs were flown by the US Coast Guard and the US Army received and still operates a number of CH-34A and CH-34C Choctaws. S-58s were also supplied to the armed forces of Argentina, Brazil, Canada, Chile, Germany, Italy, Israel, Japan, the Netherlands and Thailand. A total of 166 were licence-built in France by Sud-Aviation for the French Army and Navy, plus five for Belgium. Westland built the type in the UK, as the Wessex (which see), and exported Wessex helicopters to Australia, Ghana and Iraq.

Civil S-58s, with the same 1,525 hp Wright R-1820-84 piston engine as the Sikorsky-built military versions, were also operated in the USA and abroad. On August 19, 1970, the first flight took place of a Sikorsky prototype S-58T with an 1,800 shp PT6T-3 Twin-Pac turbine engine. By early 1975, 116 production conversions or kits for modifying existing S-58s to turbine power had been delivered, the conversion kit with the later PT6T-6 engine having been available since 1974. A Mk II conversion is now available, based on the later engine and introducing numerous other improvements, including some to the airframe.

Sikorsky S-61A and S-61B (H-3 Sea King)   USA

Anti-submarine, transport and general-purpose helicopters, in production and service.

Data: SH-3D Sea King
Powered by: Two 1,400 shp General Electric T58-GE-10 turboshafts
Rotor diameter: 62 ft 0 in (18.90 m)
Fuselage length: 54 ft 9 in (16.69 m)
Empty weight: 11,865 lb (5,382 kg)
Gross weight: 18,626 lb (8,449 kg)
Max speed: 166 mph (267 km/h)
Range: 625 miles (1,005 km)
Accommodation: Crew of four
Armament: Homing torpedoes, depth charges, etc, up to 840 lb (381 kg) weight

Photograph: Agusta-Sikorsky SH-3D of Italian Navy, with AS.12 missiles

On September 23, 1957, Sikorsky was awarded a contract by the US Navy to produce an amphibious anti-submarine helicopter that would be both "hunter and killer". The prototype made its first flight on March 11, 1959, and deliveries to the Navy, as HSS-2s, began in September 1961. The designation of the initial production aircraft, powered by 1,250 shp General Electric T58-GE-8B engines, was changed to SH-3A Sea King in the following year. Sikorsky built 255 SH-3As, and Mitsubishi of Japan had delivered 59 similar licence-built HSS-2s and 2As (S-61Bs and S-61B-1s) for anti-submarine work with the JMSDF by 1975, with the expectation of building 48 more. Conversion of a number of US Navy SH-3As has led to other Navy versions, including the RH-3A for mine countermeasures work, of which nine were delivered in 1965 for use on land and on board two ships; the HH-3A search and rescue version with T58-GE-8F engines, of which 12 were produced;

the SH-3G utility version, of which 105 were produced; and the SH-3H multi-purpose version for ASW and missile defence duties. Ten specially-equipped S-61s, designated VH-3As, are operated by the Executive Flight Detachment for VIP transport, and also offer evacuation flight capability for top government personnel, from Washington, in an emergency. Five are operated by the US Army and five by the Marine Corps. Eleven VH-3Ds are being delivered, however, to replace the VH-3As. Forty-one CH-124s (similar to SH-3As) were acquired by the Canadian Armed Forces from 1963, of which 36 were assembled in Canada.

The current standard anti-submarine version of the S-61 in service with the US Navy is the SH-3D, which first appeared in 1965. Powered by T58-GE-10 engines and carrying 140 US gallons of extra fuel, 72 have been delivered to that service. In addition, 22 SH-3Ds have been delivered to Spain, four to Brazil and four to Argentina (S-61D-4s). Since 1967, Agusta of Italy has been building Sikorsky SH-3Ds for service in Italy and Iran. These include anti-submarine, rescue, transport and VIP variants. Agusta has also built a derivative of the SH-3D designated S-61A-4. Powered by two T58-GE-5 engines, it can carry up to 31 equipped troops, 15 stretchers or freight.

Westland Helicopters of the UK has built versions of the SH-3D for the Royal Navy and for export (which see). Nine S-61A amphibious transport helicopters (similar to SH-3A) have been acquired by the Royal Danish Air Force for long-range air/sea rescue, and the Royal Malaysian Air Force received 16 S-61A-4 Nuri helicopters for troop and freight transport duties. One S-61A transport helicopter was purchased by Construction Helicopters and six CH-3Bs (S-61As) are operated by the US Air Force for missile site support and drone recovery work.

SH-3H (for details see page 63)

Sikorsky S-61L and S-61N   USA

All-weather commercial helicopters, in service.

Data: Mk II versions
Powered by: Two 1,350 shp General Electric CT58-110 turboshafts on original model, two 1,500 shp General Electric CT58-140-2 turboshafts on Mk IIs (to which the performance figures relate)
Rotor diameter: 62 ft 0 in (18.90 m)
Length (S-61N, including fore and aft rotors): 72 ft 10 in (22.20 m)
Empty weight (S-61L): 11,704 lb (5,309 kg)
Empty weight (S-61N): 12,510 lb (5,674 kg)
Gross weight (FAA): 19,000 lb (8,620 kg)
Gross weight (CAA): 20,500 lb (9,300 kg)
Max speed: 146 mph (235 km/h)
Range (S-61N): 495 miles (797 km) with reserves
Accommodation: Crew of three and up to 30 passengers in S-61L, 26-28 in S-61N. Over 11,000 lb (4,990 kg) of cargo can be carried by the Payloader (see below)

Photograph: (above) S-61L Mk II of New York Airways

These commercial developments of the Sikorsky Sea King are in service with operators in the United States and abroad. The S-61L is for land operation only and differs from its military counterparts in having a modified wheel landing gear, stabiliser and rotor head, and, like the S-61N, a longer fuselage. The first flight of an S-61L took place on December 6, 1960, and examples have been purchased by several operators, including Los Angeles Airways and New York Airways. The S-61N, which made its initial flight on August 7, 1962, is the amphibious version, retaining stabilising floats. S-61Ns have been purchased by many operators, including All Nippon Airways, Ansett-ANA, British Airways Helicopters, Bristow, the Canadian Ministry of Transport, Elivie, Greenlandair, JAL, KLM, Nitto Airways, and San Francisco and Oakland Helicopter Airlines.

Originally, CT58-110 engines were standard in both models, but these have been replaced by CT58-140-2s in the Mk II versions, which also feature greater seating capacity, better vibration damping and other improvements. A total of 88 S-61L/Ns had been delivered by January 1976.

A third version of the helicopter, called the Payloader, is basically a stripped S-61N with a fixed main landing gear, replacing the sponsons, and other changes. It weighs approximately 10,500 lb (4,762 kg) empty and has been developed for general construction and other heavy-lift work.

Photograph: (above) S-61N Mk II

Sikorsky S-61R (H-3, Jolly Green Giant/Pelican)　　USA

Troop transport, assault and rescue helicopter, in service.

Data: CH-3E
Powered by: Two 1,500 shp General Electric T58-GE-5 turboshafts
Rotor diameter: 62 ft 0 in (18.90 m)
Fuselage length: 57 ft 3 in (17.45 m)
Empty weight: 13,255 lb (6,010 kg)
Gross weight: 22,050 lb (10,000 kg)
Max speed: 162 mph (261 km/h)
Range: 465 miles (748 km)
Accommodation: Crew of two or three plus 30 troops, 15 stretchers or 5,000 lb (2,270 kg) of cargo

Photograph: (above) HH-3E Jolly Green Giant

The prototype S-61R made its maiden flight on June 17, 1963, and was developed as a general-purpose helicopter for the US Air Force. Derived from the SH-3A, it introduced many modifications, including a hydraulically-operated rear loading ramp, new stabilising sponsons, a built-in gas-turbine auxiliary power unit and other improvements. The initial production version was the CH-3C, the first of which flew a few weeks after the S-61R prototype, powered by two 1,300 shp T58-GE-1 turboshaft engines. The first order for 22 CH-3Cs, placed by the US Air Force on February 8, 1963, was followed by contracts for 19 more after the type had been selected, in the following July, to fulfil the role of long-range rotary-wing support system. Delivery of the CH-3C began on December 30, 1963. In February 1966, production was switched to the CH-3E version, powered by 1,500 shp engines, for which a pod-mounted turret armament system was developed. Forty-two new CH-3Es were built, and all the CH-3Cs were subsequently converted to this standard. Later, 50 CH-3Es were converted into HH-3Es for the US Air Force Aerospace Rescue and Recovery Service, with defensive armament, armour, self-sealing and jettisonable fuel tanks, and a rescue hoist. These are known as Jolly Green Giants. Two of them made the first non-stop crossing of the Atlantic by helicopters, on May 31-June 1, 1967. In 1968, delivery started of 40 HH-3F Pelicans for the US Coast Guard, for extended search and rescue missions. Although similar to the HH-3E, they are unarmed and have no armour or self-sealing tanks, but are fitted with advanced electronic equipment designed for this role. Agusta of Italy started licence manufacture of the HH-3F in 1974, and 20 were laid down initially for service with the Italian Navy and foreign customers.

Photograph: (above) HH-3F Pelican

Sikorsky S-62 and HH-52A   USA

Commercial transport helicopter (S-62), and search and rescue helicopter (HH-52A), in service.

Data: HH-52A
Powered by: One 1,250 shp General Electric T58-GE-8 (civil CT58-110-1) turboshaft (derated to 730 shp)
Rotor diameter: 53 ft 0 in (16.16 m)
Fuselage length: 44 ft 6 ½ in (13.58 m)
Gross weight: 8,100 lb (3,674 kg)
Max speed: 109 mph (175 km/h)
Range: 474 miles (763 km)
Accommodation: Crew of two or three and up to 12 passengers or freight

The prototype S-62A made its first flight on May 14, 1958, and the type was built subsequently in both commercial and military versions. It was Sikorsky's first amphibious helicopter, embodying the dynamic components and major systems of the earlier S-55, although the general configuration was completely new in comparison with earlier types. The turbine engine, because of its small size and weight, could be mounted above the fuselage, enabling the S-62 to be designed with a larger cabin. The S-62B is similar to the S-62A but is fitted with an S-58 main rotor that has been reduced in size to that of the S-55. Final commercial variant is the S-62C, which is similar to the HH-52As of the US Coast Guard. The latter are used by the Coast Guard for search and rescue missions and were used for the recovery of some Apollo astronauts following "splash down". In all, about 50 S-62s were built for commercial use. The US Coast Guard has about 99 HH-52As, and other S-62s were delivered to the air forces of India (2), Japan (8) and the Philippines (2). The Thailand Police Department also operates two.

Sikorsky S-64 Skycrane (CH-54 Tarhe)   USA

Heavy-lift helicopter, in production and service.

Data: CH-54A
Powered by: Two 4,500 shp Pratt and Whitney T73-P-1 turboshafts
Rotor diameter: 72 ft 0 in (21.95 m)
Fuselage length: 70 ft 3 in (21.41 m)
Empty weight: 19,234 lb (8,724 kg)
Max gross weight: 42,000 lb (19,050 kg)
Max speed: 126 mph (203 km/h)
Range: 230 miles (370 km)
Accommodation: Normal crew of three plus freight or troops in interchangeable Universal Military Pods

Basically just a forward cabin and a fuselage boom which carries the engines, tall wide-track main landing gear and tail rotor system, the Sikorsky Skycrane is a highly successful helicopter which was designed to carry interchangeable pods or slung freight. The pods, which are clamped into position directly under the flat-bottomed fuselage, can each accommodate 45 equipped troops, 24 stretchers, a surgical unit or field command or communications post. The gross weight of a pod is 20,000 lb (9,072 kg).

On May 9, 1962, the first of three prototypes made its first flight, designated S-64A. The other two prototypes, similarly designated, were sent to West Germany for evaluation by the German forces. In June 1963, the US Army ordered six Skycranes as YCH-54As. Redesignated CH-54As, five of them were used to evaluate the heavy lift concept as an aid to battlefield mobility. They were delivered to the 478th Aviation Company from June 1964 and, following their great success in supporting the Army in Vietnam, that service ordered about 60 production CH-54As. As well as airlifting troops, armoured vehicles, combat equipment and other heavy machinery, the CH-54As retrieved more than 380 damaged aircraft in Vietnam. In 1969, the US Army received two improved Skycranes under the designation CH-54B, followed by eight more in 1970/71. These were each powered by two 4,800 shp Pratt and Whitney T73-P-700 engines and were fitted with high-lift rotor blades. Gross weight for the CH-54B was increased to 47,000 lb (21,318 kg). Nine Class E-1 international helicopter records are held by the type, including that gained on April 12, 1972, when a payload of 15,000 kg was lifted to 10,850 ft (3,307 m).

Although most of the 96 Skycranes built by mid-1974 were for the US Army, others have been purchased for commercial operation. On April 18, 1969, Rowan Drilling Company received two Skycranes to support the exploration of oil in Alaska. The Erickson Air-Crane Company acquired the first of an improved civil S-64E Skycrane in early 1972 and bought three more in 1972/73. These can carry external freight weighing up to 20,000 lb (9,072 kg). Others are operated by Evergreen Helicopters and by Tri-Eagle. Civil Skycranes are also used by the logging, powerline, shipping and general construction industries. Although not yet in production, a commercial version of the improved military CH-54B Skycrane has been developed.

In both civil and military versions of the Skycrane, the third crew member sits facing the rear of the cabin and has duplicate flying controls. He is able to take control of the helicopter from this position during loading and unloading operations.

Sikorsky S-65A (H-53 Sea Stallion) and S-65 (MCM) USA

Heavy assault transport helicopter and mine countermeasures helicopter, in production and service.

Data: CH-53D
Powered by: Two 3,925 shp General Electric T64-GE-413 turboshafts
Rotor diameter: 72 ft 3 in (22.02 m)
Fuselage length: 67 ft 2 in (20.47 m)
Empty weight: 23,485 lb (10,653 kg)
Max gross weight: 42,000 lb (19,050 kg)
Max speed: 196 mph (315 km/h)
Range: 257 miles (413 km)
Accommodation: Crew of three and up to 55 troops, 24 stretchers or internal or external freight

Photograph: (above) HH-53C

Using experience gained with the S-64 Skycrane, Sikorsky designed the S-65 to meet a US Marine Corps requirement for a heavy assault transport helicopter. The prototype made its first flight on October 14, 1964, under the designation CH-53A, and deliveries of production CH-53A Sea Stallions, each with two 2,850 shp General Electric T64-GE-6 engines, started in 1966. By the beginning of the following year, the type was operational in Vietnam. The main duty of CH-53As is to carry freight, such as two Jeeps, a 1½-ton truck and trailer, two Hawk missiles and equipment, or a 105 mm howitzer. Rear cargo doors under the tail-boom provide access to the freight cabin, loading being facilitated by a hydraulically-operated freight handling system and floor rollers. The fuselage itself is sealed and provided with sponsons to permit emergency landings on water. In April 1968, a CH-53A performed the first automatic terrain clearance flight by a helicopter, and later completed tests of an Integrated Helicopter Avionics System. In the same year a Sea Stallion was involved in flight investigations during which it was looped and rolled. In June 1967, the first of eight armed HH-53Bs were delivered to the USAF Aerospace Rescue and Recovery Service. Powered by 3,080 shp T64-GE-3 turboshafts, they introduced external jettisonable fuel tanks, a retractable in-flight refuelling probe and a rescue hoist. At the end of August 1968, the USAF took delivery of the first of many improved HH-53Cs, each powered by 3,925 shp T64-GE-7 engines. These have an external cargo hook with a capacity of 20,000 lb (9,070 kg). A total of 72 HH-53Bs and Cs were built by Sikorsky.

Between March 1969 and January 1972, the US Marine Corps received an improved version of the CH-53A, designated CH-53D. By the end of CH-53D production, the Marines had received 265 Sea Stallions. The German forces acquired 113 similar CH-53Gs, powered by T64-GE-7 engines; these were assembled and partially manufactured in Germany, VFW-Fokker being the German prime contractor. Iran ordered six S-65As for its Navy; Israel bought eight CH-53s; and the Austrian Air Force has two S-65-Oe helicopters, delivered in 1970, with accommodation for 38 passengers, for rescue duties in the Alps. In September 1973, initial deliveries were made of 30 RH-53Ds for the US Navy. These are specially equipped for minesweeping and follow 15 CH-53As that the US Navy had borrowed for mine countermeasures duties under the designation RH-53A. Two 3,780 shp General Electric T64-GE-413A engines were fitted in the first examples built — to be converted later by kits into 4,380 shp T64-GE-415 turboshafts. The RH-53D is able to sweep mechanical, acoustic and magnetic mines, using special equipment, and has provision for two 0.50 in machine-guns to detonate mines on the surface. Maximum gross weight of this version is 50,000 lb (22,680 kg) and it has an endurance of more than four hours. Six have been delivered to Iran. (See also the Sikorsky YCH-53E.)

Under the designation S-65C, Sikorsky is proposing a commercial inter-city helicopter based on the CH-53. Differences include a longer nose section and larger sponsons. It would carry about 44 passengers, or could be configured for 30 passengers or cargo for off-shore platform operations. An existing CH-53 is under test as part of the development programme.

Photograph: (above) CH-53G
Photograph: (below) RH-53D towing magnetic
mine-sweeping equipment
(Details of both types on page 69)

Sikorsky S-72　　　　　　　　　　　　　　　　　　　USA

High-speed multi-purpose research helicopter.

Powered by: Two 1,500 shp General Electric T58-GE-5 turboshafts. Two auxiliary 9,275 lb (4,205 kg) st General Electric TF34-GE-2 turbofans optional

Rotor diameter: 62 ft 0 in (18.90 m)

Wing span: 45 ft 1 in (13.74 m)

Empty weight as helicopter: 14,490 lb (6,572 kg)

Gross weight as helicopter: 18,400 lb (8,346 kg)

Gross weight (compound): 26,200 lb (11,884 kg)

Max speed: about 345 mph (555 km/h)

Accommodation: Crew of three

Known officially as Rotor Systems Research Aircraft (RSRA), two prototypes of this helicopter have been built by Sikorsky, for use by NASA and the US Army, to develop and evaluate a range of rotors and integrated propulsion systems. The S-72 will be able to fly in three different ways—as a helicopter, as a compound helicopter using auxiliary engines, and as a fixed-wing aircraft. The last two configurations are produced by fitting to the basic helicopter detachable wings and auxiliary turbofan engines, mounted on the fuselage sides. One set of wings and a pair of podded engines were ordered at the same time as the two aircraft, and have a dual purpose. As well as enabling the helicopter to test rotor systems that would otherwise be too small to keep it airborne, they make possible aircraft-type take-offs and landings, and provide the crew with a flyable aircraft should the rotor under test fail. For further safety, a mechanical system will back up the fly-by-wire controls of the aircraft.

The contract to build the two S-72s and auxiliary wings, and to provide the two Lockheed Viking-type podded turbofan engines, was awarded to Sikorsky in January 1974. The first flight of an S-72 was expected to take place in August 1976, and about 80 hours of flight testing will be conducted by Sikorsky before the aircraft are handed over to NASA and the US Army.

Photograph: (above) Impression of completed S-72

Photograph: (below) Prototype S-72 before fitting of wings and turbofans

Sikorsky S-76

USA

General-purpose helicopter, under development.

Powered by: Two 650 shp Allison 250-C30 turbo-shafts
Rotor diameter: 44 ft 0 in (13.41 m)
Fuselage length: 44 ft 1 in (13.44 m)
Empty weight: 4,942 lb (2,241 kg)
Gross weight: 9,700 lb (4,399 kg)
Max cruising speed: 178 mph (286 km/h) at 8,400 lb (3,810 kg) AUW
Range: 461 miles (742 km) with full passenger load
Accommodation: Crew of two and up to twelve passengers, with a baggage hold of 42 cu ft (1.19 m³), or up to 5,000 lb (2,268 kg) of externally-slung freight, or other equipment for varied roles including rescue and ambulance

Photograph: Mockup of S-76

Sikorsky has, for many years, concentrated on larger helicopters, mainly for military applications, and it has been left to Bell Helicopter Textron and others to produce smaller civil helicopters in the USA. To extend its share of the market, Sikorsky Aircraft has decided to produce a medium-capacity transport helicopter specifically for civil operators. However, by constructing it to the highest standards laid down by the most exacting civil or military specification, the company expects that the S-76 should lend itself to military application without modification to main components such as the rotor system and drive or the basic airframe. As with the projected S-78, the S-76 will incorporate features developed for the S-70 (YUH-60A) military Utility Tactical Transport Aircraft System helicopter, including a scaled-down replica of the UTTAS main four-blade rotor, which has swept tips. The first orders for the S-76 have already been received from Okanagan Helicopters Ltd and Island Helicopters Inc, although the first flight of the helicopter is not scheduled until May 1977, with first deliveries of fully-certificated IFR (instrument flight) aircraft in July 1978.

Sikorsky S-78   USA

20/29-passenger commercial helicopters, under development.

Data: S-78-20
Powered by: Two 1,420 shp General Electric T700 turboshafts
Rotor diameter: 53 ft 0 in (16.15 m)
Fuselage length: 50 ft 11 ½ in (15.53 m)
Empty weight: 9,126 lb (4,139 kg)
Gross weight: 17,520 lb (7,947 kg)
Max speed: about 193 mph (311 km/h)
Range: 460 miles (740 km)
Accommodation: Crew of two, plus seating for 20 passengers or up to 12,000 lb (5,443 kg) of externally-slung freight

Photograph: Artist's impression of S-78-20 (foreground) and S-78-29

As a further bid to gain more of the civil helicopter market, Sikorsky has projected two civil variants of its S-70 (YUH-60A) military helicopter which is being developed for the US Army. Many of the advanced features of the S-70 will be embodied in the civil version, including the four-blade main rotor with swept tips, elastomeric rotor hub bearings that do not require lubrication, and greased and sealed intermediate and tail rotor gearboxes.

Two versions of the S-78 are projected—a 20-seat model as described above, and a 29-seat version which will incorporate several improvements over the smaller-capacity helicopter. It will, for example, have an extra 6 in (15 cm) of headroom and 5 ft 3 in (1.6 m) longer passenger cabin, making the cabin 5 ft (1.5 m) high and 21 ft 6 in (6.55 m) long. The maximum speed of the larger-capacity S-78-29 is expected to be similar to that of the S-78-20, partly through the use of a retractable undercarriage, although its maximum take-off weight will be 19,997 lb (9,070 kg).

Sikorsky YCH-53E

USA

Heavy multi-purpose helicopter, under development.

Powered by: Three 4,380 shp General Electric T64-GE-415 turboshafts
Rotor diameter: 79 ft 0 in (24.08 m)
Fuselage length: 73 ft 9 in (22.48 m)
Empty weight: 32,048 lb (14,537 kg)
Max gross weight: 69,750 lb (31,638 kg), with external load
Max speed: 196 mph (315 km/h)
Range: 306 miles (492 km)
Accommodation: Crew of three and up to 55 troops, or internal or external freight (internal payload 8 tons and external payload 14.4 tons over short distances)

The YCH-53E has been developed for the US Navy and Marine Corps, the first prototype making its maiden flight on March 1, 1974. It is a three-engined development of the Sikorsky S-65A, introducing a new seven-blade main rotor, with titanium blades, and many other changes, including an uprated transmission and modified tail surfaces. Production aircraft will have in-flight refuelling capability, an advanced automatic flight control system, an all-weather navigation system and long-range fuel tanks. The first prototype was destroyed in a ground accident, but the programme has been continued with the second prototype, which flew on January 21, 1975. Following successful initial evaluation and testing of this prototype, two pre-production YCH-53Es and one static test airframe were built. The pre-production models began flying at the end of 1975. Production of the CH-53E will depend upon the success of the tests carried out with these later types, and the decision whether or not to go ahead was expected to be made in 1976.

In service, the type would be used by the Navy to deliver cargo on board ship, to back up mobile construction units, and to lift damaged aircraft from the decks of aircraft carriers. In support of the Marine Corps, the helicopter would be able to carry 93 per cent of a division's combat gear and could also be used to recover damaged aircraft.

Sikorsky YUH-60A (S-70)   USA

Utility transport helicopter, under development.

Powered by: Two 1,536 shp General Electric T700-GE-700 turboshafts
Rotor diameter: 53 ft 0 in (16.15 m)
Gross weight: 22,000 lb (9,979 kg)
Cruising speed: 184 mph (296 km/h)
Accommodation: Crew of three and 11 troops, four stretchers or internal or external freight (7,000 lb/3,175 kg external freight hook)
Armament: Side-firing machine-gun can be carried

The US Department of Defense announced on August 30, 1972, that contracts had been awarded to Sikorsky and Boeing Vertol, for each to build three prototype helicopters under the US Army's UTTAS (Utility Tactical Transport Aircraft System) programme. The Sikorsky YUH-60A was first to fly, on October 17, 1974, the second and third prototypes following on January 21 and February 28, 1975, respectively. Powered by the same engines as the Boeing Vertol contender, the YUH-60A differs mainly in having advanced main rotor blades with titanium spars, glassfibre skins and swept tips, a canted tail rotor and a non-retractable tailwheel-type undercarriage. It has been designed in such a way that six YUH-60As could be carried in a Lockheed C-5A Galaxy transport aircraft.

As with the Boeing Vertol YUH-61A, a commercial variant of the YUH-60A is being developed, under the designation S-78 (which see). In addition, a modified version of the YUH-60A is being produced as a contender for the US Navy's Mk III LAMPS (Light Airborne Multi-Purpose System) programme. The main changes in the LAMPS variant are provision for the rotor blades to be folded automatically, movement of the tailwheel further forward, fitting of MAD and surface search radar, and provision for carrying two Mk 46 torpedoes.

Silvercraft SH-4

Italy

General-purpose and agricultural helicopter, in production and service.

Powered by: One 235 hp Franklin 6A-350-D1B piston engine (derated to 170 hp)
Rotor diameter: 29 ft 7 ½ in (9.03 m)
Fuselage length: 25 ft 1 ¼ in (7.65 m)
Empty weight: 1,142 lb (518 kg)
Gross weight: 1,900 lb (862 kg)
Max speed: 100 mph (161 km/h)
Range: 200 miles (320 km)
Accommodation: Pilot and two passengers, agricultural equipment including spraybars and chemical tanks with a capacity of up to a weight of 441 lb (200 kg), externally-slung freight of up to 441 lb (200 kg) total weight, or one stretcher carried externally in a pannier.

Developed from the Silvercraft XY, the first product of Silvercraft SpA, the SH-4 prototype made its first flight in March 1965. It was followed by five pre-production aircraft, and the type was certificated by the RAI and FAA in the following year, becoming the first all-Italian helicopter to gain such approval. Fiat's Aero-Engine Division is producing components for the rotor transmission system of the initial batch of 50 production aircraft, deliveries of which started in 1970. The helicopter is being produced in two major forms for operators in Italy and abroad, as the SH-4 and SH-4A. The former is a general-purpose version and can be used for both civil and military duties, including general transport, ambulance, survey, flight training, police, observation and liaison work. The SH-4A is an agricultural version, fitted with 32 ft 9 ½ in (10.00 m) spraybars and related equipment. Two hundred more SH-4s are expected to be built during the next phase of production.

Westland 606

Great Britain

Commercial general-purpose helicopter, under development.

Powered by: Two 900 shp Rolls-Royce Gem 2 or Pratt and Whitney (Canada) PT6B-34 turboshafts, limited to a total of 1,385 shp
Rotor diameter: 42 ft 0 in (12.80 m)
Fuselage length: 43 ft 10 in (13.36 m)
Gross weight: 9,500 lb (4,309 kg)
Max cruising speed: 161 mph (259 km/h)
Range: 230 miles (370 km) with 2,204 lb (1,000 kg) payload
Accommodation: Crew of one or two, and 12/13 passengers, or three stretchers, four sitting casualties and an attendant, 5/8 passengers in VIP configuration, or freight

Photograph: Mockup of Westland 606

The Westland 606 is basically a civil version of the Lynx military general-purpose helicopter, differing mainly in having a longer fuselage, Rolls-Royce Gem 2 or Pratt and Whitney engines and commercial-type accommodation. Development is being carried out by Westlands as a private venture, and a full-size mockup was built initially. Standard equipment will include automatic stabilisation equipment, a three-axis autopilot and blind-flying instrumentation. The main rotor will be capable of running in negative pitch. Optional features will include automatic transition from cruise to hovering flight, an external cargo hook, a rescue hoist and other equipment for a variety of roles. One of the major applications which the manufacturers foresee for the helicopter is in support of offshore oil and gas platforms.

Westland Commando

Great Britain

Tactical transport, support and rescue helicopter, in production and service.

Data: Commando Mk 2
Powered by: Two 1,590 shp Rolls-Royce Gnome H.1400-1 turboshafts
Rotor diameter: 62 ft 0 in (18.90 m)
Fuselage length: 55 ft 10 in (17.02 m)
Empty weight: 12,222 lb (5,543 kg)
Gross weight: 21,000 lb (9,525 kg)
Max speed: 137 mph (220 km/h)
Range: 298 miles (480 km) with 28 troops; 120 miles (193 km) with a 6,000 lb (2,720 kg) externally-slung load
Accommodation: Crew of two plus up to 28 troops, internal or external freight or stretchers
Armament: Provision for a variety of guns, missiles, etc

Photograph: Commando Mk 2

Intended primarily as a troop or freight transport, logistic support and casualty evacuation helicopter, the Commando can also be used for ground attack or search and rescue missions. Announced in 1971, it is based on the Westland Sea King. Five Commando Mk 1s were ordered by Saudi Arabia, on behalf of Egypt. The first two of these made their maiden flights in September 1973 and were delivered to Egypt in February 1974. The Mk 1s have accommodation for 21 troops and are fitted with a retractable landing gear. They differ externally from the Sea King mainly in absence of the search radar that the Sea King carries in a dome above the centre-fuselage. The more-specialised and major production version, the Commando Mk 2, has a fixed undercarriage and other changes. The first Mk 2 flew on January 16, 1975, and 19 were ordered under the initial contract from Saudi Arabia. The Qatar Emiri Air Force has also received three Commando Mk 2 troop transports and one VIP transport.

Westland Sea King   Great Britain

Anti-submarine and general-purpose helicopter, in production and service.

Data: Sea King HAS. Mk 2
Powered by: Two 1,660 shp Rolls-Royce Gnome H.1400-1 turboshafts
Rotor diameter: 62 ft 0 in (18.90 m)
Fuselage length: 55 ft 9¾ in (17.01 m)
Empty weight: 13,413 lb (6,084 kg)
Gross weight: 21,000 lb (9,525 kg)
Cruising speed: 129 mph (208 km/h)
Range: 764 miles (1,230 km) with standard fuel
Accommodation: Crew of four in anti-submarine role. Provision for up to 22 persons, or nine stretchers and two attendants, in SAR role
Armament: Four Mk 44 homing torpedoes, four Mk 11 depth charges or bombs, etc. Machine-gun can be carried in starboard doorway of cabin

Photograph: Sea King Mk 41

The Sea King was developed originally for the Royal Navy as an anti-submarine helicopter. Development of the HAS. Mk 1 version began after a licence agreement had been concluded with Sikorsky, in 1959, which allowed Westland Helicopters to build the SH-3D (S-61) in a modified form. Changes included the installation of two 1,500 shp Rolls-Royce Gnome H.1400 engines, an automatic flight control system of the type used in the Wessex HAS. Mk 3, long-range sonar with Doppler processing and bathythermograph facilities, a tactical display provided by AW391 search radar and an associated Doppler navigation system. The first production model made its initial flight on May 7, 1969, and delivery of 56 HAS. Mk 1s was completed by May 1972. The first Sea King unit was No 700S Squadron, Royal Navy, commis-

sioned on August 19, 1969. An uprated version of the Sea King for the Royal Navy is the HAS. Mk 2; deliveries of the thirteen examples ordered for ASW and SAR began in 1976. These have uprated engines and transmissions and other improvements, permitting a take-off weight some 500 lb (225 kg) greater than that of the first version. Fifteen similar Sea King HAR. Mk 3s have been ordered for SAR duties with the RAF.

Westland-built Sea Kings have been exported to several countries, including 22 Sea King Mk 41s for search and rescue missions with the Federal German Navy; twelve Sea King Mk 42 anti-submarine helicopters for the Indian Navy; ten Sea King Mk 43 search and rescue helicopters for the Norwegian Air Force; six Sea King Mk 45 anti-submarine helicopters for the Pakistan Navy; and five Sea King Mk 48s for the Belgian Air Force, for search and rescue missions. The export versions are generally similar to the Royal Navy Mk 1, but the Royal Australian Navy ordered 10 Sea King Mk 50s incorporating many of the improvements found in the Royal Navy's Mk 2 version. Deliveries to Australia began in late 1974 and these aircraft operate (as do the Royal Navy's Sea Kings) in a variety of roles, including anti-submarine, tactical troop transport, search and rescue, vertical replenishment and casualty evacuation. The uprated Sea King can carry up to 6,000 lb (2,720 kg) of cargo internally, or 8,000 lb (3,630 kg) externally, in the transport role. Other layouts provide for various mixed combinations of equipment, passenger seats, stretchers and cargo.

Westland Wasp and Scout

Great Britain

Anti-submarine helicopter (Wasp) and liaison helicopter (Scout), in service.

Data: Wasp
Powered by: One 710 shp Rolls-Royce Bristol Nimbus 503 turboshaft (derated)
Rotor diameter: 32 ft 3 in (9.83 m)
Fuselage length: 30 ft 4 in (9.24 m)
Empty weight: 3,452 lb (1,566 kg)
Gross weight: 5,500 lb (2,495 kg)
Max speed: 120 mph (193 km/h)
Range: 270 miles (435 km) at 110 mph (177 km/h)
Accommodation: Crew of two, with provision for three passengers or stretcher
Armament: Two Mk 44 homing torpedoes or other stores carried externally

Photograph: (above) Scout of Uganda Police Air Wing

These helicopters, developed initially for the Royal Navy and British Army, were derived from the Saunders-Roe P.531. This had been built as a private venture, the first of two prototypes flying on July 20, 1958, powered by a 325 shp Turmo engine. The Royal Navy evaluated one of these prototypes and two similar helicopters, which led to the development and eventual production of the Wasp HAS. Mk 1. A prototype P.531, powered by a Nimbus engine, flew for the first time on August 9, 1959; and on October 28, 1962, the first production Wasp took to the air. This also had a Nimbus engine, and a folding tailboom and four-leg undercarriage with castering wheels. Deliveries to the Navy began in 1963. The Royal Navy ordered approximately 80 Wasp HAS. Mk 1s, and these are used as anti-submarine helicopters from *Tribal*, *Leander* and *Rothesay* class frigates. Others were

ordered by the navies of Brazil (3), the Netherlands (12), New Zealand (3) and South Africa (17). Production of the Wasp ended in 1974, but examples continue in service with the Royal Navy and are to be equipped with APX Bézu M.260 gyro-stabilised periscopic weapon sights.

The Westland Scout differs from the Wasp in having a fixed tail and a skid undercarriage, and is powered by a 685 shp Nimbus 101 or 102 turboshaft engine. The first pre-production Scout, ordered by the Army Air Corps, made its maiden flight on August 4, 1960. The Army ordered approximately 150 Scout AH. Mk 1s, the first flying on March 6, 1961. Other operators of the Scout are the Royal Australian Navy, which has two for survey work, and the Uganda Police Air Wing.

Photograph: (above) Wasp HAS Mk 1 with AS 12 missile

Westland Wessex

Great Britain

Anti-submarine and military and commercial transport helicopter, in service.

Data: Wessex HU. Mk 5
Powered by: One Rolls-Royce Gnome 112 and one Gnome 113 turboshafts, coupled to give output of 1,550 shp
Rotor diameter: 56 ft 0 in (17.07 m)
Fuselage length: 48 ft 4 ½ in (14.74 m)
Empty weight: 8,657 lb (3,927 kg)
Gross weight: 13,500 lb (6,120 kg)
Max speed: 132 mph (212 km/h)
Range: 478 miles (770 km)
Accommodation: Crew of one to three, and 16 troops, seven stretchers or 4,000 lb (1,814 kg) of freight
Armament: Provision for SS.11 air-to-surface missiles, torpedoes, rocket launchers and machine-guns

Photograph: Wessex Mk 1 equipped for search and rescue duties

Westland produced a large number of single- and twin-engined helicopters for civil and military use under the name Wessex. Development of the Wessex began in 1956, when Westland acquired a licence from Sikorsky to build the S-58 and also received a Sikorsky-built HSS-1 (SH-34). Following its arrival in the UK, the HSS-1 was re-engined with an 1,100 shp Gazelle N.Ga.11 turboshaft engine and first flew in this configuration on May 17, 1957. The first of two pre-production aircraft flew on June 20, 1958, and deliveries to the Royal Navy of production HAS. Mk 1 anti-submarine helicopters began in 1960. Powered by a 1,450 shp Gazelle 161 engine and fitted with a large dorsal radome,

dipping sonar and associated armament, the Wessex HAS. Mk 1 was commissioned with its first squadron in July of the following year. In 1962, the Commando assault carrier HMS *Albion* received a 16-seat assault transport version of the Mk 1 helicopter. Meanwhile, on January 18, 1962, a Wessex made its first flight powered by two coupled Gnome engines, and the first production aircraft with a similar power plant took to the air on October 5. Production aircraft to this standard for the RAF were designated HC. Mk 2s.

The HAS. Mk 3 variant of the Wessex is similar to the Mk 1 but is powered by a 1,600 shp Gazelle 165 turboshaft engine. Two Mk 2 helicopters were converted into HCC. Mk 4s and are used by The Queen's Flight. A Commando assault version of the Mk 2 for the Royal Navy, designated HU. Mk 5, first flew on May 31, 1963. Altogether the RAF received about 60 HC. Mk 2s and 2 HCC. Mk 4s, and the Navy received approximately 150 HAS. Mk 1, HAS. Mk 3 and HU. Mk 5 Wessex. The Royal Australian Navy acquired 27 Wessex HAS. Mk 31Bs, powered by 1,540 shp Gazelle 162 engines, and other military versions included Wessex 52s for the Iraqi Air Force, Wessex 53s for the Ghana Air Force, Wessex 54s for Brunei and two Wessex HC. Mk 5s for Bangladesh.

Fifteen commercial Wessex series 60 helicopters (basically similar to the Mk 2) were built by Westlands, most of which remain in service, notably with Bristow Helicopters.

Westland/Aérospatiale Lynx

Great Britain/France

Multi-purpose military helicopter, in production and service.

Data: Lynx HAS. Mk 2 (anti-submarine)
Powered by: Two Rolls-Royce BS.360-07-26 Gem turboshafts
Rotor diameter: 42 ft 0 in (12.80 m)
Fuselage length: 39 ft 1 ¼ in (11.92 m)
Empty weight (equipped): 6,797 lb (3,083 kg)
Gross weight: 9,500 lb (4,309 kg)
Max continuous cruising speed: 170 mph (273 km/h)
Range: 391 miles (629 km)
Accommodation: Basic crew of two; or pilot and 10 troops, 2,000 lb (907 kg) of internal freight, 3,000 lb (1,360 kg) of external freight, or three stretchers and an attendant. Other layouts available for different roles
Armament: Provision for one 20 mm AME 621 cannon or similar gun, or 7.62 mm GEC Minigun inside cabin, or Minigun beneath cabin. Two Mk 44 or Mk 46 homing torpedoes and six marine markers, or two Mk 11 depth charges. All versions can carry racks for two Minigun or other gun pods, rockets, or six Hawkswing or AS.11, or eight Hot or TOW missiles, or Sea Skua semi-active homing missiles, or AS.12s

Photograph: Lynx HAS Mk 2

In accordance with an Anglo-French agreement, five Lynx prototypes were constructed under the design leadership of Westland. Before the first had flown, on March 21, 1971, two Westland Scout light helicopters had tested scaled-down replicas of the Lynx rotor system. All five prototypes had flown by April 12, 1972; that date marking the first flight of a Lynx in British Army configuration. A sixth Lynx was delivered initially to Rolls-Royce for engine development, and seven more were produced for military development of the helicopter. The first of these was the initial Royal Navy prototype HAS. Mk 2, which first flew on May 25, 1972; the third was the initial French Navy prototype which flew on July 6, 1973. By the late spring of 1975, over 2,000 flying hours had been recorded by Lynx helicopters. The initial production order was placed in 1973, and in early 1976 the Royal Navy had 30 on order, the British Army 63 and the French Navy 18. In addition, 16 Lynx have been ordered by the Royal Netherlands Navy and the Brazilian Navy has ordered nine.

The Lynx AH. Mk 1 for the British Army is scheduled to enter service in late 1976. This version can be used for a variety of tasks, including anti-tank attack, tactical troop transport, helicopter escort, reconnaissance, logistic support, search and rescue, evacuation and command post work. The first Royal Navy HAS. Mk 2s were also scheduled for delivery during 1976, equipped with Ferranti Seaspray search and tracking radar. The Mk 2s will be used as frigate-borne anti-submarine hunter-killer helicopters, and for anti-surface vessel, reconnaissance, search and rescue, liaison, vertical replenishment, fire support, communications and troop transport duties. The French Navy Lynx is generally similar to that of the Royal Navy, but has more advanced target detection equipment. A training version for the RAF has been projected as the Lynx HT. Mk 3. During a series of record attempts on June 20/22, 1972, the first prototype Lynx AH. Mk 1 achieved a speed of 199.92 mph (321.74 km/h) over a 15/25 km course.

A version of the helicopter known as the Sea Lynx has been projected by Westland as a contender for the US Navy's LAMPS competition, and as such will be matched against several American helicopters as a successor to the Kaman Seasprite. A commercial version of the Lynx is the Westland 606 (which see).

Lynx AH Mk 1

WSK-Swidnik Mi-2 and Mi-2M
(NATO code-name: Hoplite)

Poland

General-purpose civil and military helicopter, in production and service.

Data: Mi-2
Powered by: Two 400/450 shp Isotov GTD-350 turboshafts, built in Poland
Rotor diameter: 47 ft 6¾ in (14.50 m)
Fuselage length: 37 ft 4¾ in (11.40 m)
Empty weight: 5,213-5,344 lb (2,365-2,424 kg)
Gross weight: 8,157 lb (3,700 kg)
Max speed: 130 mph (210 km/h) at 1,650 ft (500 m)
Range: 105 miles (170 km) with standard fuel, max payload
Accommodation: Pilot and eight passengers, four stretchers and a medical attendant, agricultural equipment, externally-slung freight, rescue equipment or armament
Armament: Mi-2 has been seen with air-to-surface rocket packs

Photograph: Mi-2 equipped for agricultural duties

The Mi-2 was developed initially in the USSR, as a successor to the Mi-1, but the Polish WSK-Swidnik works was entrusted with final development and production. By replacing the Mi-1's piston engine with two lightweight turboshafts, mounted above the cabin, the Mi-2 was enabled to carry a payload about 2½ times that of the earlier helicopter. The prototype first flew in 1962, and in September of the same year was demonstrated to Soviet officials. The first Polish-built Mi-2 was flown in November 1963 and, following tests, production started there in 1965/66. Production aircraft were powered at first by 400 shp engines, but the Mi-2 was uprated to 450 shp when a new version appeared in 1974. Another version followed, with rotor blades, tail rotor and stabiliser of plastics.

Several hundred Mi-2s have been built for both civil and military use. In the former roles they are used as passenger and freight transports (the latter carrying a sling-load of up to 1,763 lb/800 kg or internal freight), agricultural helicopters with spray-bars and two hoppers, trainers, ambulances, and for aerial television camera work. In the military role Mi-2s are operated by several countries, including Bulgaria, Czechoslovakia, Hungary, Poland, Romania and the USSR.

A further development of the helicopter is the Mi-2M, production of which started in 1975. This has a wider and higher cabin to accommodate nine passengers or freight, and other improvements, including use of the 450 shp engine as standard.

SECOND SECTION

Aerospace General Mini-Copter

USA

Three prototypes of this ultra-light helicopter have been ordered by the US Navy for evaluation as pilot rescue vehicles. Intended to be air-dropped to stranded pilots in enemy territory or in hostile terrain, the Mini-Copter can be folded to fit into a US Navy CTU/1A aerial delivery container, measuring 5 ft long by 2 ft wide (1.52 m × 0.61 m), and can be reassembled for flight by the pilot to be rescued in around a minute. Power for the rotor is provided by rotor-tip rockets (42 lb/19 kg thrust each), and control is by a handle-grip throttle stick positioned ahead of the pilot. A single-blade counterbalanced anti-torque rotor is mounted at the tail, forward of a Vee tail surface. **Data:** Empty weight about 125 lb (57 kg). Gross weight about 550 lb (250 kg). Max speed 110 mph (177 km/h). Range about 20 miles (32 km).

Aérospatiale AS 350 Ecureuil

France

Intended to replace the Alouette series, the AS 350 Ecureuil (Squirrel) is a five/six-seat helicopter which flew for the first time on 27 June 1974, powered by a 600 shp Avco Lycoming LTS 101 turboshaft (F-WVKH). A second prototype (F-WVKI), with 650 shp Turboméca Arriel turboshaft, flew in February 1975. Production Ecureuils, available in 1978, will be offered with choice of either power plant. Plastics are used extensively throughout the airframe, and for the main rotor blades and 'Starflex' simplified hub. **Data:** Rotor diameter 35 ft 0¾ in (10.69 m). Length 35 ft 9½ in (10.91 m). Gross weight 4,190 lb (1,900 kg). Max speed (LTS 101) 159 mph (256 km/h). Range (LTS 101) 510 miles (820 km).

Aerotechnik WGM 22

Germany

Developed from the three WGM 21 single-seat prototypes, the WGM 22 is a projected two-seat helicopter of unusual design. The four two-blade rotors are mounted at the ends of supporting arms, which are positioned on top of the rotor column. The engine is located in the rear of the fuselage. This layout makes a tail rotor or tail control surfaces unnecessary. The cabin, which accommodates two persons side by side, is totally glazed except for the rear bulkhead and floor, and the helicopter has a tricycle undercarriage. So far, only a mockup of the WGM 22 has been produced. **Data:** Max speed about 124 mph (200 km/h). Range about 497 miles (800 km).

Agusta-Bell 205 and 205A-1

Italy

Agusta has produced under licence many Bell
Model 205 utility helicopters for military service
with the armed forces of Iran, Italy, Kuwait,
Morocco, Saudi Arabia, Spain, Turkey, the United
Arab Emirates, and Zambia. The Model 205 is
basically a UH-1D/UH-1H and can be equipped for
several roles, including tactical support, troop
transport, evacuation, ambulance and rescue. It
can be fitted with different undercarriages and can
be armed. The commercial version is designated
Agusta-Bell 205A-1, corresponding to the Bell
205A-1, and has been in production since 1969.
Powered by a 1,400 shp Lycoming T5313B
turboshaft (derated to 1,250 shp), it provides
normal accommodation for a pilot and up to 14
passengers, with alternative layouts for executive,
ambulance, flying crane and freight carrier
(9,500 lb/4,310 kg T-O weight with internal or
external cargo) configurations. **Data (205A-1):**
Rotor diameter 48 ft 0 in (14.63 m). Length 41 ft
11 in (12.78 m). Max gross weight 10,500 lb
(4,762 kg) with external load. Max speed 138 mph
(222 km/h). Range 331 miles (532 km).

Bell H-13 Sioux   USA

Versions of the Bell Model 47 were built in the USA under the name Sioux, for military service in the USA and abroad, and were also built under licence by Westland and Agusta. The US Army still has approximately 16 OH-13 Sioux helicopters in service for observation duties and around 150 for training, as TH-13s. These basic designations cover several versions including the OH-13G and TH-13M, which are derived from the civil Bell 47G and powered by 200 hp Franklin 6V4-200-C32 engines; the OH-13H, based on the Bell 47G-2, with the 240 hp Lycoming VO-435 engine; the three-seat OH-13S, derived from the Bell 47G-3B and powered by the 260 hp TVO-435-25 engine; and the TH-13T instrument trainer, derived from the Bell 47G-3B-1 and powered by the 270 hp TVO-435-25 engine. Westland-built Sioux helicopters were based on the Bell 47G-3B-1. In British Army service the Sioux is designated AH. Mk 1 and approximately 250 are operational. With the RAF the type is designated HT. Mk 2. Agusta of Italy licence-built the Sioux for the Italian Air Force, Navy and Army, with which about 90, 12 and 120 are in service

respectively, and also built the type for other customers. Users of Sioux helicopters include Argentina, Austria, Brazil, Burma, Chile, Colombia, Ecuador, Greece, Guinea, India, Indonesia, Japan, Malaysia, Mexico, Morocco, New Zealand, Pakistan, Paraguay, Peru, Spain, Sri Lanka, Taiwan, Tanzania, Turkey, Uruguay, Venezuela, Zaire and Zambia. **Data (47G-3B-1):** Rotor diameter 37 ft 1 ½ in (11.32 m). Length 31 ft 7 in (9.63 m). Gross weight 2,950 lb (1,338 kg). Max speed 105 mph (169 km/h). Range 315 miles (507 km).

Photograph: Sioux AH Mk 1

Bell Model 222

USA

The Bell Model 222 is a light commercial helicopter, powered by two 600 shp Avco Lycoming LTS 101-650C turboshaft engines. Able to accommodate ten persons in a high-density layout, six persons in an executive layout, freight, or two stretchers and two attendants, in addition to the crew, the Model 222 embodies Bell's focused pylon and nodalisation concept to reduce vibration. Other design features include a retractable undercarriage, stub wings which carry the main undercarriage units, dual electrical and hydraulic systems, fail-safe structures and various additional safety features. The Model 222 has been designed to comply with FAR Part 29 Transport Category specifications, and a full-scale mockup was put on view in 1974. First flight of the prototype was expected in spring 1976, and deliveries to operators should begin about two years later. **Data:** Rotor diameter 39 ft 0 in (11.89 m). Length 39 ft 9 in (12.12 m). Gross weight 6,700 lb (3,039 kg). Max speed 180 mph (290 km/h). Range 425 miles (685 km).

Bell Model 301 (XV-15)　　　　　　　　　　　USA

The Bell Model 301 is a tilt-rotor research aircraft, developed under a contract from the NASA Ames Research Center and the US Army's Air Mobility Research and Development Laboratory. Two examples are being built, with the first flight of one of the aircraft scheduled for late 1976. The Model 301 (US Army and NASA designation XV-15) is basically an aircraft with a fixed forward-swept wing and two wingtip-mounted 1,800 shp Lycoming LTC1K-4K (T53) turboshaft engines that can be operated in both horizontal and vertical positions. The large rotors are stiff in plane and gimbaled, with an elastomeric hub spring to enhance control power and damping; the blades themselves are of high-twist design. In operation, the aircraft will take off vertically as a helicopter and, at a safe height, swivel the engines gradually to a horizontal position for forward flight. When completed, the first Model 301 will be tested in the full-size wind tunnel at NASA's Ames Research Center, before joining the second aircraft for flight testing. The programme is aimed at proving the design practical, finding out its operational limits,

and providing data for projected future larger civil and military aircraft of similar concept. **Data:** Rotor diameter (each) 25 ft 0 in (7.62 m). Gross weight (VTOL) 13,000 lb (5,897 kg). Max speed about 415 mph (667 km/h). Cruising speed 345 mph (556 km/h).

Photograph: (above) Projected military version
Photograph: (below) Prototype

Bell Model 409 (YAH-63)　　　　　USA

In November 1972, the US Army issued a request for proposals for a new Advanced Attack Helicopter. All major helicopter manufacturers in America participated, and the Army eventually chose the Bell and Hughes Helicopters designs for further development. Each of these two manufacturers was contracted to build two flying prototypes and one ground test vehicle of its design, for evaluation by the Army from May 1976. The Bell design (US Army designation YAH-63) is powered by two 1,536 shp General Electric T700-GE-700 turboshaft engines and has a low-profile, upper and lower tail fin arrangement, with a horizontal surface at the apex. Stub wings are fitted to the fuselage, and the crew of two sit in tandem, with the pilot in the front cockpit. A zero g main rotor hub is fitted, with flapping axis moment springs, and there are nodalised dynamic beams in the rotor pylon suspension system. Armament consists of TOW anti-tank missiles or 2.75 in rockets, and a three-barrel 30 mm cannon which is carried under the helicopter's nose. An infra-red vision system will permit night firing of TOW. Testing of the ground test vehicle began at Bell's Arlington Experimental Flight Test works on April 19, 1975, and the two flying prototypes made their first flights on October 1 and December 21, 1975, respectively. **Data**: Gross weight 15,000 lb (6,805 kg). Cruising speed 167-202 mph (269-325 km/h). Endurance over 1 ¾ hours.

Boeing Vertol Model 179　　　　　USA

The Model 179 is basically a commercial version of the YUH-61A military helicopter that Boeing Vertol designed for the US Army's UTTAS programme and which first flew on November 29, 1974 (which see). Incorporating many of the advanced features developed for the military helicopter, the prototype Model 179 was rolled out on May 23, 1975, and made its maiden flight on August 5. Production aircraft will accommodate between 14 and 20 passengers, and will have IFR capability. Twenty-eight Model 179s have been ordered by Petroleum Helicopters Inc. **Data**: Rotor diameter 49 ft 0 in (14.94 m). Length 51 ft 8¾ in (15.77 m). Gross weight 18,700 lb (8,482 kg). Max cruising speed 184 mph (296 km/h). Range 598 miles (963 km).

Boeing Vertol/ MBB BO 105 Executaire

USA

Since 1972, Boeing Vertol has possessed rights to market the German MBB BO 105 helicopter in the US, and up to mid-1975 had sold nearly fifty. It also holds the rights to construct and market the helicopter for sale in the US and other western countries. Under this agreement, Boeing Vertol has produced a modified version of the BO 105 known as the Boeing Vertol BO 105 Executaire, which flew for the first time on March 18, 1975. The Executaire differs from the standard BO 105 in having a 10 in (0.25 m) longer rear passenger cabin, hinged instead of sliding rear doors, and extra windows for the rear passengers, and can accommodate the pilot and up to five passengers in a utility configuration. **Data:** Rotor diameter 32 ft 2¾ in (9.82 m). Length about 28 ft 10½ in (8.80 m). Empty weight 2,504 lb (1,136 kg). Gross weight about 5,100 lb (2,316 kg).

BredaNardi NH-500

Italy

The BredaNardi company was formed in February 1971, by the Breda and Nardi companies, to manufacture under licence the Hughes Model 300C and 500C helicopters and their derivatives. Production began in 1974 with manufacture of the Model 300C, 500C five-seat commercial helicopter and 500M military helicopter, as the NH-300C, NH-500C, and NH-500M/MC respectively. The company also plans to put in production an anti-submarine version of the 500M designated NH-500ASW. **Data:** see Hughes Model 500.

CW Helicopter Research CW 205

Belgium

The CW 205 is a light helicopter that has been designed for production in both completed and kit form, the latter for home construction. It is a side-by-side three-seater, powered by a 245 hp Lycoming O-435 engine which drives two counter-rotating and intermeshing four-blade rotors. The blades of each rotor are mounted in pairs, separated by an angle of only 10° instead of the customary 90°, so that the rear blade of each pair acts as a kind of "Fowler flap" for the front one. The fully-enclosed streamlined fuselage is of metal construction, with access to the cabin via a sliding one-piece Plexiglas canopy. Twin sweptback tail fins are mounted at the tips of a variable-incidence tailplane, fitted with elevators. The undercarriage is retractable. Construction of the prototype CW 205 was started in December 1973. **Data:** Rotor diameter (each) 23 ft 9 in (7.24 m). Length 20 ft 8 in (6.30 m). Gross weight 2,381 lb (1,080 kg). Max cruising speed 149 mph (240 km/h). Range 373 miles (600 km).

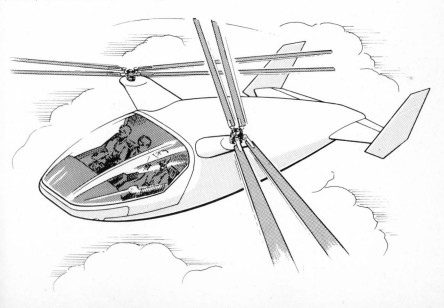

Cicaré CH-III Colibri

Argentine Republic

Cicaré Aeronáutica SC was formed in 1972 to produce light helicopters and aero-engines. Following experimental prototypes known as the Cicaré I and II, the company has now built a prototype of the CH-III, which was scheduled to fly for the first time in early 1976. Its design was started in August 1973, under an Argentine Air Force contract, for potential use as a light training and agricultural helicopter. Looking somewhat like the US Hughes Osage, the Colibrí is a two- or three-seater with a four-blade rigid main rotor. Glassfibre has been used extensively in its construction, notably for the main and tail rotor blades, cabin and tail stabilisers. Power plant is a 190 hp Lycoming HIO-360-D1A piston engine. Max payload is 500 lb (226 kg); optional equipment includes agricultural gear and a cargo sling. **Data:** Rotor diameter 24 ft 6 in (7.47 m). Length overall 28 ft 0 in (8.53 m). Gross weight 1,764 lb (800 kg). Max speed 101 mph (163 km/h). Range 298 miles (480 km).

Photograph: CH-II

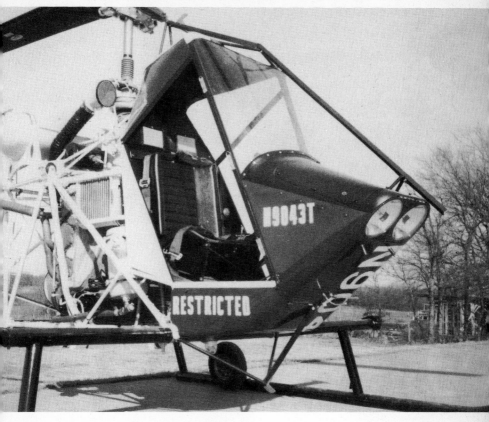

Continental Copters El Tomcat Mk V-A

USA

Developed specifically for agricultural purposes, from 1959 onwards, the various versions of the El Tomcat single-seat helicopter are converted Bell Model 47s, stripped of unnecessary structure and equipment to increase payload capacity, and fitted with revised control systems compatible with their new role. The El Tomcat Mk V-A is a modified Bell Model 47G-2, powered by a 260 hp Lycoming VO-435-A1F engine. The simple cab which has replaced the original cabin was improved in 1974 by the introduction of a pilot "cage", comprising a rigid forward frame to the cockpit. A modified glassfibre nose allows easy access to all instruments, the battery and other equipment, and also houses two in-flight-adjustable landing lights. A jump-seat is provided for a passenger. Operational safety has been enhanced by the installation of a wire or cable deflector and cutter system. The chemical spray tanks are installed against the fuselage, aft of the pilot's cab. **Data:** Rotor diameter 37 ft 1½ in (11.32 m). Gross weight 2,450 lb (1,111 kg). Range 100 miles (160 km).

Continental Copters El Tomcat Mk VI-B

USA

Based on the Bell Model 47G-5, the El Tomcat Mk VI-B superseded the Mk VI, of which only the prototype was completed, and is now the standard production version. It is powered by a 270 hp Lycoming TVO-435-B1A engine, and has a similar pilot "cage" to that of the Mk V-A. Additional equipment includes a compass and an altimeter. Three examples have been delivered to Portugal.

Airframe kits for the Mk V-A and the Mk VI-B are obtainable, with operators supplying their own Bell 47 power packs. Conversion kits for the Mk VI-B installation are also available. **Data:** Gross weight 2,850 lb (1,293 kg). Maximum speed 70 mph (113 km/h).

Hughes YAH-64   USA

Under the US Army designation YAH-64, Hughes has designed an Advanced Attack Helicopter (AAH) to meet an Army requirement for the late 1970s. Like Bell Helicopter Textron, Hughes was contracted to build two flight test prototypes and one for ground tests. The first prototype flew on September 30 and the second on November 22, 1975. Competitive evaluation of the Hughes and Bell aircraft was scheduled to begin in 1976. Powered by two 1,536 shp General Electric T700-GE-700 turboshafts, the YAH-64 carries a crew of two in tandem, with the pilot at the rear. The main legs of the tailwheel-type undercarriage fold aft to reduce height for storage and transport. Like its Bell counterpart, the YAH-64 has been designed primarily as an anti-tank aircraft, although close support missions will also be possible. Armament comprises a Hughes 30 mm chain gun in an underfuselage turret, underwing attachments for eight TOW missiles and two packs of 2.75 in rockets, or 76 rockets without TOWs. There is an

infra-red system for night operations. **Data:** Rotor diameter 48 ft 0 in (14.63 m). Gross weight 17,400 lb (7,892 kg). Max speed 191 mph (307 km/h). Endurance 3.2 hours.

Kaman H-43 Huskie

USA

The original version of the Huskie was the HOK-1, with intermeshing rotors and "bear paw" landing feet, ordered by the US Navy in 1950. Later redesignated OH-43D, this was a five-seater, powered by a piston engine. It was used by the US Marine Corps in Korea to post patrols and to string telephone wires. The US Air Force ordered the same basic type in HH-43A, HH-43B and HH-43F versions. Eighteen piston-engined HH-43As were acquired first, followed by the major version, the HH-43B. This switched to an 825 shp Lycoming T53-L-1B turboshaft engine, and the USAF received 193 examples. Final USAF version was the HH-43F (described below), of which 40 were bought, the 1,150 shp Lycoming T53-L-11A turboshaft engine (derated to 825 shp) giving a big power reserve for operations at high altitudes and/or in hot climates. The USAF Huskies were used mainly for firefighting and rescue work at airfields, but have now been replaced by Bell UH-1Ns. The USAF HH-43Fs had accommodation for a pilot and two firefighters and 1,000 lb (454 kg) of firefighting or rescue equipment, four stretchers and an attendant, or a crew of two and 10 passengers. A drone variant of the HH-43F was produced as the QH-43G for the US Navy.

HH-43Bs were also supplied to Burma (12), Colombia (6), Morocco (4), Pakistan (6) and Thailand (3). Iran received 17 HH-43Fs. Many of these remain in service. **Data (HH-43F):** Rotor diameter (each) 47 ft 0 in (14.33 m). Length 25 ft 2 in (7.67 m). Gross weight 9,150 lb (4,150 kg). Max speed 120 mph (193 km/h). Range 504 miles (811 km).

MBB BO 105HGH

Germany

The BO 105HGH is a high-speed helicopter that was built originally for research flying by conversion of a pre-production BO 105. Initial modifications included a rear fuselage extension that faired the otherwise rounded rear fuselage into the tailboom, a circular rotor head fairing, and four small undercarriage skids in place of the normal twin-skid unit. In this configuration, the BO 105HGH flew at 231 mph (372 km/h) in September 1973. This represented an increase in maximum speed of about 60 mph (97 km/h) compared with the standard model. Flying was resumed in the following year after straight fixed wings had been attached to the fuselage and a shorter under-carriage fitted. The wings are tapered in chord towards the tips and are fitted with airbrakes above and below the leading-edges. With them, maximum speed was raised by a further 20 mph (32 km/h). The BO 105HGH test programme ended in March 1975, and the helicopter is now being used as a testbed for rotor blades. Power is provided by two 400 shp Allison 250-C20 turbo-shafts. **Data:** Rotor diameter 32 ft 2¾ in (9.82 m). Length 28 ft 0½ in (8.55 m). Span of fixed wings (when fitted) 19 ft 8¼ in (6.00 m). Max speed 251 mph (404 km/h).

MBB BO 106

Germany

This helicopter is an enlarged version of the BO 105 with accommodation for up to seven persons, and was built with the assistance of the German government. Changes from the BO 105 include a wider cabin to make room for the extra seats, uprated 420 shp Allison 250-C20B engines, and an uprated transmission to allow a total output of up to 692 shp. The prototype made its first flight on September 25, 1973, and, in addition to new production, MBB plans to produce kits to convert BO 105s to BO 106 standard.

Mil Mi-1 and WSK-Swidnik SM-1

USSR/Poland

First flown in September 1948, the Mi-1 was the first helicopter produced in series in the USSR. Production aircraft were built for both military and civil use (NATO code name "Hare") and military versions are still in service with several forces, including those of Afghanistan, Albania, Algeria, Cuba, Czechoslovakia, East Germany, Iraq and Mongolia. The standard seating was for four persons, but variants of the Mi-1 included the three-seat Mi-1T, the Mi-1U dual-control trainer, Mi-1 Moskvich for Aeroflot, and the multi-purpose Mi-1NKh with attachments for two stretcher panniers, agricultural equipment (the hoppers being positioned on the sides of the cabin), mail carrying containers, and external fuel tanks. Mi-1 production was transferred to the Polish WSK-Swidnik works in 1955, and large numbers were built under the designation SM-1. A single 575 hp Ivchenko AI-26V piston engine was the standard power plant in all of these helicopters. **Data** (**Mi-1NKh**): Rotor diameter 46 ft 11 in (14.30 m). Length 39 ft 4¾ in (12.01 m). Gross weight 4,960 lb (2,250 kg). Max speed 118 mph (190 km/h). Range 236 miles (380 km).

Photograph: SM-1 ambulance version

Nagler Model 202

USA

This somewhat unusual-looking two-seat helicopter is the projected production version of the
earlier Nagler Honcho 200, itself a derivative of the
Honcho 100. Power for the rotor is provided by
tip-mounted cold-jets, which derive their thrust
from the 225 hp T-100 bleed air compressor. The
fuselage is of welded steel tube construction with a
glassfibre outer shell, and supports a large tail unit
comprising dorsal and ventral fins and a rudder, the
latter mid-positioned in the efflux from the
compressor. First flight of the Model 202 was made
in January 1975. **Data:** Rotor diameter 36 ft 0 in
(10.97 m). Length overall 10 ft 0 in (3.05 m). Gross
weight 1,400 lb (635 kg). Max speed 120 mph (193
km/h). Range 240 miles (386 km).

Phillips Phillicopter Mk 1

The Phillicopter, designed by Mr D. A. Phillips and Mr P. Gerakiteys, is a two-seat light helicopter powered by a 145 hp Rolls-Royce Continental O-200-C engine. The basic structure is of steel tube, with a cabin of aluminium and glassfibre. Construction of the prototype began in 1967, five years after design work started, and the prototype made its first flight in 1971. Orders for production Phillicopters have been received, but manufacture of these had not started in early 1976, as flight trials had not been completed. **Data:** Rotor diameter 25 ft 6 in (7.77 m). Length 21 ft 10 in (6.65 m). Gross weight 1,650 lb (748 kg). Max speed 90 mph (145 km/h). Range 230 miles (370 km).

Robinson R22

First product of the Robinson Helicopter Company of Torrance, California, the R22 is a side-by-side two-seat lightweight helicopter designed with the emphasis on high efficiency, low noise and minimum maintenance requirements. The prototype, powered by a 115 hp Lycoming O-235-C2A piston engine, flew for the first time on August 28, 1975, about two years after its design was started. By the end of the year it had completed 35 hours of testing, including all normal flight manoeuvres at speeds up to 100 mph (161 km/h). It is hoped to receive FAA type approval in time for production to begin in mid-1977. Cost is intended to be comparable with that of two-seat and four-seat lightplanes. **Data:** Rotor diameter 25 ft 2 in (7.67 m). Length 20 ft 8 in (6.30 m). Gross weight 1,230 lb (558 kg). Max cruising speed 100 mph (161 km/h). Range approximately 250 miles (400 km).

RotorWay Scorpion and Scorpion Too

USA

The RotorWay Scorpion was in production for several years as a lightweight single-seat helicopter and was sold in kit form to amateur constructors. Since production ended, RotorWay Inc has marketed the larger two-seat Scorpion Too. The company offers to potential builders both plans and a complete helicopter in kit form, although plans and the rotor are offered by themselves to constructors who wish to use their own materials. For builders with limited money, RotorWay has available small breakdown kits which allow the constructor to build the helicopter in stages and so spread the cost over a period of time. Additional help is available from the company in the form of advice during the construction phase and pre-flight training. The Scorpion Too is powered by a 140 hp Vulcan V-4 engine which drives a two-blade semi-rigid main rotor. The fuselage is of steel tube construction with a glassfibre outer shell. **Data (Scorpion Too)**: Rotor diameter 24 ft 0 in (7.32 m). Length 20 ft 3½ in (6.18 m). Gross weight 1,125 lb (510 kg). Cruising speed over 75 mph (121 km/h). Range 125 miles (201 km).

Photograph: Scorpion Too

Scheutzow Bee and Hawk 140

USA

Following development of a new type of rotor head, known as a "Flexhub", on a test helicopter, three prototypes of the projected production version of the Bee were built. The first of these made its maiden flight in 1966, and the prototypes proved highly successful in both hovering and autorotative trials. The main rotor, which incorporates a control gyro-bar, is driven by a 180 hp Lycoming IVO-360-A1A engine and features the Scheutzow "Flexhub". Good manoeuvrability and control are provided by the elastomeric bearings, with an offset flapping hinge. It was expected that the Bee would receive its FAA Type Certification in 1976, in which year production was scheduled to begin. Accommodation is for two persons, and optional equipment includes agricultural equipment, a stretcher arrangement and dual controls. **Data:** Rotor diameter 27 ft 0 in (8.23 m). Length 24 ft 1 in (7.34 m). Gross weight 1,685 lb (764 kg). Max speed 93 mph (150 km/h). Range 175 miles (280 km) with standard fuel.

The Hawk 140 was designed in 1974 as a low-drag lightweight helicopter, with dynamic components of similar type to those used on the Bee. Power will be provided by a modified Lycoming O-320 engine. If production goes ahead, the Hawk 140 will be offered to amateur constructors in kit form.

Photograph: Bee

Seremet W.S.8

Denmark

The W.S.8 is the latest helicopter produced by Mr W. Vincent Seremet, who has been building and testing small helicopters since the early 1960s. It is a one-man strap-on helicopter, of which testing began in 1975. Although few details are known, it can be seen to stand on tripod legs for easy fitting to the pilot, and has a two-blade main rotor and a two-blade tail rotor mounted at the end of a short boom. Control is by two handgrips which extend forward from the main structure.

Sikorsky S-67 Blackhawk

USA

Design of the Sikorsky Blackhawk high-speed attack helicopter began in the latter half of 1969 as a private venture. The prototype made its first flight on August 20, 1970, and completed its initial trials in the following month. On December 14 and December 19, 1970, the Blackhawk set up world speed records in Class E1 over 3 km and 15/25 km courses, flying at up to 216.844 mph (348.971 km/h). With a new ducted tail rotor the Blackhawk achieved 230 mph (370 km/h) in a dive in 1974, but the more conventional tail rotor was subsequently reinstated. The prototype was destroyed in an accident at the 1974 Farnborough Air Show and the future of the helicopter is at present unknown.

Sikorsky S-69 (XH-59A)

USA

Sikorsky built two research aircraft, designated XH-59A, under contract from the US Air Mobility Research and Development Laboratory, to flight test the Advancing Blade Concept (ABC) rotor system. This consists of two co-axial counter-rotating three-blade rotors, which make full use of the aerodynamic lift of the blades on the advancing side of each rotor disc, without adverse effect by the retreating blade. The first prototype made its maiden flight on July 26, 1973, but was involved in an accident in August of the same year. The accident led to several modifications to the design, and the second prototype (first flown on July 21, 1975) embodies these alterations, which included changes to the aircraft's control system. At present the XH-59A is powered by one Pratt and Whitney (Canada) PT6T-3 Turbo Twin Pac, but provision has been made for the later fitting of two auxiliary P & W J60 turbojets in fuselage side-mounted pods. **Data:** Rotor diameter 36 ft 0 in (10.97 m). Length 40 ft 9 in (12.42 m). Max design speed as helicopter 196 mph (315 km/h). Max design speed with J60 engines 345 mph (555 km/h).

SELECTED AUTOGYROS

AISA Autogyro GN   Spain

Although not scheduled for prototype flight tests until 1977, plans have been under way since 1970 for this new autogyro with jump take-off capability, able to accommodate a pilot and three passengers. The design incorporates a fully-enclosed fuselage with short-span wings, the latter supporting the main undercarriage legs; twin tailbooms, elevator, horizontal tailplane and twin large-area fins and rudders; and a four-blade articulated rotor; and is powered by a 300 hp Lycoming IO-540-K1A5 engine. **Data:** Rotor diameter 42 ft (12.80 m). Length 21 ft 4 in (6.50 m). Gross weight 2,645 lb (1,200 kg). Max speed 149 mph (240 km/h). Range 497 miles (800 km).

Photograph: Model of Autogyro GN

AMR XR 200/XR 207

USA

Powered by a 75 hp light aircraft engine, the AMR XR 200 is a prototype autogyro with normal accommodation for two persons. The engine drives a rear-mounted Benson External Rotorduct, although vertical take-off can be achieved by the engine driving the rigid two-blade main rotor and then being disengaged for forward flight. Because of the Rotorduct, no anti-torque or stabilising devices are necessary. However, a rear-mounted fin and rudder are fitted. **Data:** Max speed 160 mph (257 km/h).

Scheduled to fly in 1976, the XR 207 is a projected production aircraft developed from the XR 200. It will accommodate five persons in a fully enclosed and streamlined fuselage which reduces in size aft of the rotor pylon to form the tailboom on which is fitted a single fin and rudder. Small curved delta wings will be fitted to the fuselage sides to off-load the three-blade rigid main rotor, behind which are two Benson Rotorducts driven by two Continental engines. **Data:** Design max speed about 230 mph (370 km/h).

Photograph: (top) XR 207
Photograph: (above) XR 200

Barnett J-3M and J-4B

USA

These are two ultra-light single-seat gyroplanes of similar basic design, which are available to home constructors in the form of plans, materials and kits of parts. Each has a two-blade wooden rotor, with steel spar and glassfibre covering. The J-3M is a utility model, powered by a 65 hp Continental A65 engine and with a flat-sided fabric-covered cabin. The higher-performance J-4B is a more demanding aircraft to build, with a streamlined glassfibre nacelle, optional cockpit canopy, and an 85 hp Continental C85 engine. **Data:** Rotor diameter 23 ft 0 in (7.01 m). Length overall (J-3M) 11 ft 4 in (3.45 m); (J-4B) 12 ft 2 in (3.71 m). Gross weight (J-3M) 650 lb (294 kg); (J-4B) 750 lb (340 kg). Max speed (J-3M) 85 mph (137 km/h); (J-4B) 115 mph (185 km/h). Range (J-3M) 120 miles (193 km); (J-4B) 250 miles (402 km).

Photograph: (above) J-3M
Photograph: (right) J-4B

111

Bensen Model B-8 Gyro-Glider

USA

Many hundreds of these simple unpowered rotor gliders are in existence, built either by the designers, Bensen Aircraft Corporation, or by amateur constructors from kits or plans.

Requiring no pilot's licence in the USA, the B-8 can be towed by a small car and has also achieved free gliding. Single- or two-seat pilot-trainer versions are available, the latter being equipped with a wide-track castering crosswind landing gear. In addition, the USAF is experimenting with single and two-seat versions of the Gyro-Glider, designated X-25. The aim is to test the feasibility of incorporating a set of folding rotor blades, together with the normal parachute, into an ejection rescue system, known as a Discretionary Descent Vehicle (DDV), which would enable a pilot to select a landing site within gliding range. A floatplane version of the B-8 is known as the Hydro-Glider.
Data: Rotor diameter 20 ft (6.10 m). Length 11 ft 4 in (3.45 m).

Bensen Model B-8M, B-8V and Super Bug Gyro-Copters and B-8MW Hydro-Copter

USA

Designed for amateur construction from kits or plans, the Gyro-Copter is a powered autogyro conversion of the Gyro-Glider. The first production Model B-8M flew initially on October 9, 1957, three months after the first flight of its prototype. It has a more powerful engine than the earlier B-7M Gyro-Copter, being equipped with a 72 hp McCulloch Model 4318E engine (a 90 hp McCulloch 4318G is optional). A mechanical rotor drive is also available which will drive the rotor to flying speed while the aircraft is stationary; or a 1 hp Ohlsson & Rice Compact III two-stroke engine can be fitted to the rotor for prerotation, cutting out at take-off rpm. Various non-standard items offered include a larger-diameter rotor, and a floor-type control column in place of the standard overhead type. Moreover, the B-8M can be rendered completely roadworthy simply by locking the rotor in a fore and aft position.

The B-8V is basically similar to the B-8M but is fitted with a 64 hp Volkswagen engine. Details for converting the B-8M to B-8V standard or for mounting the Volkswagen engine on to a basic B-8 airframe are available.

An advanced version of the B-8M, known as the Super Bug, was introduced in 1971. A special twin-engine installation spins up the rotor before take-off and is claimed to be the intermediate step to full VTOL capability. Other additions to the standard equipment are made, including a rotor brake.

A further version is the Hydro-Copter, a Gyro-Copter fitted with twin floats. **Data (Model B-8M)**: Rotor diameter 20 ft 0 in (6.10 m) or 22 ft 0 in (6.70 m). Length 11 ft 4 in (3.45 m). Gross weight 500 lb (227 kg). Max speed 85 mph (137 km/h). Range 100 miles (160 km).

Photograph: Hydro-Copter

Bensen Model B-8MA Agricopter

USA

Equipped specifically for agricultural purposes, the B-8MA is another version of the B-8M and was first flown in September 1969. Fitted with a 5 US gallon (19 litre) tank for ultra-low-volume chemicals beneath the engine, the Agricopter is capable of treating an area of between 160-400 acres during a 40-minute flight. Applications of the Agricopter are planned to include aerial survey and forest and pipeline patrol, although it is currently certificated only in an Experimental (Market Survey) category by the FAA. **Data:** Rotor diameter 21 ft 8 in (6.60 m). Length 13 ft 3 in (4.04 m). Gross weight 600 lb (272 kg). Max speed 85 mph (137 km/h). Range 100 miles (160 km).

Bensen Model B-16S Gyro-Copter

USA

Described as the world's first flying snowmobile, the B-16S is a developed version of the basic B-8M, fitted with twin 48 hp Kiekhaefer KAM 525 snowmobile engines. Special features include ski landing gear, a large-diameter rotor, tail snow baffle, plastics fuel system components, gimbal head and double-tube mast. The B-16S can be converted rapidly to wheel or float configuration. **Data:** Rotor diameter 22 ft 8 ½ in (6.92 m). Length overall 11 ft 7 ¼ in (3.54 m). Gross weight 700 lb (317 kg). Max speed 80 mph (129 km/h). Range 60 miles (96 km).

Photograph: (above) Benson B-8MA
Photograph: (above right) Benson B-16S
Photograph: (below right) Benson 75

Bensen Model 75 Gyro-Copter

USA

Evolved from the Super Bug, the Model 75 introduced a fundamental change to the rotor system, in that its rotor is driven continuously by the auxiliary engine, instead of being utilised only for rotor spin-up. Claimed advantages include quick starts with full power from standstill, with a take-off run of less than 200 ft (61 m); enhanced lifting capability; no rotor slowdown during zero g manoeuvres; and a shallower glide angle when the main engine is throttled back. Control is via a floor column instead of the usual hanging stick.

CSIR SARA II

South Africa

Design of this two-seat twin-boom experimental autogyro began in March 1965. The prototype made its first free flight at Swartkop air force base on November 30, 1972, having already completed a series of tethered tests. Features of the CSIR SARA II (South African Research Autogyro) include an extensively-glazed cabin seating two crew side-by-side with dual controls, and a tail unit comprising twin fins and rudders, bridged by a fixed-incidence tailplane; the power plant consists of a 180 hp Lycoming O-360-A engine. A second, modified prototype is being built, following an accident to the first. **Data:** Rotor diameter 36 ft 6¼ in (11.13 m). Length 15 ft 3 in (4.65 m). Gross weight 1,851 lb (840 kg) (for experimental aircraft only). Max speed 95.5 mph (154 km/h).

Campbell Cricket

Great Britain

This single-seat light autogyro is powered by a 72 hp modified Volkswagen engine. It is conventional in design with a small fuselage nacelle and open cockpit, a tricycle undercarriage and a single fin and rudder. About 47 aircraft have been built since the prototype made its initial flight in July 1969. Available optional equipment includes a special camera mount for aerial photographic work and crop-spraying gear for the agricultural version which first flew on January 21, 1971, and which utilises ultra-low-volume (ULV) insecticides. **Data:** Rotor diameter 21 ft 9 in (6.63 m). Length 11 ft 3 in (3.43 m). Gross weight 600 lb (272 kg). Max speed 80 mph (129 km/h). Range 140 miles (225 km).

Ekström Humlan 2

Sweden

The Humlan 2 is a single-seat autogyro which flew for the first time in June 1975, exactly two years after its design was initiated. It has a single two-blade semi-rigid rotor, a small fuselage nacelle with open cockpit, a conventional single fin and rudder, and a fixed tailplane with dihedral. Power plant is a 90 hp McCulloch AF 100-X3 engine, driving the usual pusher propeller. **Data:** Rotor diameter 22 ft 3¾ in (6.80 m). Length overall 11 ft 2¾ in (3.42 m). Gross weight 650 lb (295 kg). Max speed 111.5 mph (180 km/h). Range 161 miles (260 km).

Farrington (Umbaugh) Model 18-A and 20-A   USA

Developed originally by the Umbaugh Aircraft Corporation in 1957-62, the Model 18-A is a two-seat light autogyro, powered by a 180 hp Lycoming O-360-A1D engine. It has a two-blade fully-articulated rotor, and a tail unit consisting of an all-moving central fin and two fixed fins at the tips of the tailplane. The version of the 18-A produced by Farrington Aircraft has several improvements, including a strengthened nose-wheel strut, a variable collective-pitch trim system, better soundproofing and a night flying kit with beacons. Existing Model 18-As can be brought up to this standard. A further-improved version is the 20-A, with a larger-diameter rotor, 200 hp Lycoming engine and other changes, which raise the max speed to 115 mph (185 km/h). Two international speed records were established by a Model 18-A in 1971, in FAI Class E3 for autogyros, with average speeds of 108.698 mph (174.932 km/h) over a 15/25 km course and 102.132 mph (164.365 km/h) over a 100 km closed circuit. **Data (18-A):** Rotor diameter 35 ft 0 in (10.67 m). Length 19 ft 10½ in (6.06 m). Gross weight 1,800 lb (816 kg). Max speed 110 mph (177 km/h). Range 200 miles (322 km).

Tervamäki-Eerola ATE-3 and JT-5 (MT5)   Finland

First flight of the prototype ATE-3 took place on May 11, 1968, following two years of design work. This single-seat light autogyro has a two-blade semi-rigid rotor and is powered by a 75 hp Volkswagen engine, modified from a motor car engine. Changes were made to the tail unit in November 1969, with the deletion of the horizontal tail surfaces and the introduction of a redesigned vertical fin and rudder.

Significant modification of the basic ATE-3 design, including the wide-ranging use of plastics in the structure and components, resulted in a developed version known as the JT-5, first flown on January 7, 1973. Other improvements include new low-drag fuselage contours; a fully-enclosed Plexiglas cockpit; and a triple-tail unit comprising a central fin and rudder and two smaller outer fins for

increased static and dynamic stability. The prototype and all production rights, tools and moulds are now held by Sr Vittorio Magni of Italy who intended to market the aircraft as the MT5.

Several ATE-3s and JT-5s are under construction by amateurs in Finland. Additionally, sets of glassfibre rotor blades and propellers of the type used on these aircraft are available for fitting to other autogyros. **Data:** Rotor diameter 22 ft 11 ½ in (7.00 m). Length (ATE-3) 10 ft 6 in (3.20 m); (JT-5) 11 ft 5 ¾ in (3.50 m). Gross weight (ATE-3) 573 lb (260 kg); (JT-5) 639 lb (290 kg). Max speed (ATE-3) 87 mph (140 km/h); (JT-5) 106 mph (170 km/h). Range (ATE-3) 185 miles (300 km); (JT-5) 217 miles (350 km).

Photograph: JT-5

Wallis WA-116 and WA-116-T   Great Britain

The prototype WA-116, first flown on August 2, 1961, with a 72 hp McCulloch 4318 engine, represented Wing Commander K. Wallis's original autogyro design. Compared with earlier designs it introduced many refinements, including a rotor head with offset gimbal system which provided full stability with hands and feet off the controls and removed pitch-up problems; a high-speed flexible rotor spin-up shaft with positive disengagement during flight; an automatic system of controlling rotor drive on take-off which allows use of full power until the last moment; and a novel safe-starting arrangment. Nine more WA-116s were built, four of them by Beagle, of which the last was converted into a two-seater, designated WA-116-T, first flown on April 3, 1969. Another WA-116 was fitted with a 60 hp Franklin 2A-120-A engine in 1971; its designation was changed to WA-116/F, and the McCulloch models were given the suffix Mc. Modifications continue to be made, including the installation of a four-blade propeller on standard WA-116/F conversions. One has been modified for long-range flights. It flew for the first

time in its new form in April 1974 and, three months later, set a world record of 416 miles (670 km) for distance around a closed circuit, in classes E3 and E3a for autogyros. The same flight set a 100 km closed-circuit speed record of 81.19 mph (130.67 km/h) and a 500 km record of 78.38 mph (126.14 km/h). On September 29, 1975, Wing Commander Wallis flew the same WA-116/F non-stop from Lydd, Kent, to Wick, Caithness, a distance of 543 miles (874 km), setting a new straight-line record for autogyros. The WA-116-T/Mc has been used in an experimental programme conducted by Plessey Radar, on behalf of the Home Office, to evaluate the possibility of detecting illicit graves from the air, using multispectral photography. **Data (WA-116/Mc):** Rotor diameter 20 ft 4 in (6.20 m). Length 11 ft 1 in (3.38 m). Gross weight 550 lb (250 kg). Max speed 115 mph (185 km/h). Range 140 miles (225 km).

Wallis WA-117/R-R

Great Britain

Photograph: (above)

Basically a WA-116 autogyro fitted with a 100 hp Rolls-Royce Continental O-200-B engine, the experimental test model of the WA-117 made its first flight on March 24, 1965. However, this was later dismantled and the first WA-117 prototype proper made its maiden flight on May 28, 1967. This aircraft features special silencers and a four-blade "quiet" propeller, and has been used for many purposes including taking part in the 1970 Loch Ness investigation. It has also been fitted with a variety of equipment including HSD Linescan 212 infra-red sensor equipment, multi-spectral, cine and still cameras. Development continues to improve further the WA-117's high-speed flight characteristics. **Data:** Gross weight about 700 lb (317 kg). Max speed 120 mph (193 km/h).

Wallis WA-118/M Meteorite

Great Britain

Photograph: (facing page upper)

Intended for a long-term test programme, this aircraft first flew on May 6, 1966, thirteen months after design work started. It was rebuilt subsequently with a reclining cockpit, canopy and other modifications, making its first flight in this new form on August 9, 1969. The Meteorite is being used as a testbed for the supercharged 120 hp Italian Meteor Alpha I engine, intended as the power plant of the small, high-altitude WA-121/M. The WA-118/M itself is expected to achieve speeds of up to 200 mph (322 km/h).

Wallis WA-120/R-R

Great Britain

Photograph: (below)

This member of the Wallis family was designed originally as the WA-117-S. The designation WA-120/R-R was adopted when it developed into much more than a WA-117 with a different engine. In its current form it has a forward-sliding cockpit canopy, a 130 hp Rolls-Royce Continental O-240-A engine and only vertical tail surfaces, the original tapered horizontal tail surfaces having proved unnecessary. First flight was made on June 13, 1971.

Wallis WA-121

Great Britain

The prototype WA-121, lightest and most compact of the Wallis autogyros, made its initial flight on December 28, 1972. Features include an open cockpit, high-mounted tailplane and the WA-117 type of special rotor head suspension. Improvements to the control system ensure better stability at speed and added comfort for the pilot. The high-speed WA-121/Mc, with 100 hp Wallis-McCulloch engine, has already exceeded unofficially the speed and altitude records held by the WA-116. Planned future versions are the WA-121/F with 60 hp Franklin 2A-120-B, and high-altitude WA-121/M Meteorite 2 with a supercharged 120 hp Meteor Alpha 1 engine.

WHE Airbuggy

Great Britain

Evolved from the McCandless Mk IV Gyroplane, the WHE Airbuggy is a single-seat light autogyro powered by a 75 hp modified Volkswagen engine, and fitted with a two-blade semi-rigid teetering rotor. The prototype flew for the first time on February 1, 1973. The aircraft is available ready built or as a kit. **Data:** Rotor diameter 21 ft 9 in (6.63 m). Length overall 11 ft 6 in (3.51 m). Gross weight 650 lb (295 kg). Max speed 80 mph (128 km/h). Range with max fuel 140 miles (225 km).

PHOTOGRAPH ACKNOWLEDGEMENTS

Australian Department of Defence, 23, 29
Peter J. Bish, 117
S. J. Cherz, 102
Alain Crosnier, 11
E.C.P. Armées, Paris, 4
Martin Fricke, 11, 15, 37, 55, 76
John Goring, 65
Howard Levy, 27
Peter R. March, 7, 80, 81
T. Matsuzaki, 28
Ministry of Defence, London, 61, 88

Stephen P. Peltz, 48, 100
Alex Reinhard, 38
Brian M. Service, 12, 14, 42, 56
South African Air Force, 6
Tass, 47, 52, 57, 59
Norman E. Taylor, 69
USAF, 98
US Navy, 29, 44
John Wegg, 48
Gordon S. Williams, 53

INDEX